THE ISSUES OF 1982:

A BRIEFING BOOK

Prepared By:

The Conference on Alternative State and Local Policies
2000 Florida Avenue, N.W.
Washington, D.C. 20009
(202) 387-6030

1982

The Conference is a national public policy center that concentrates on the problems of America's state and local governments. In meeting the needs of public officials and citizen and civic groups alike, the Conference is America's best source for new ideas for state and local government.

The Conference is the only national organization that focuses exclusively on developing progressive and innovative policy ideas and legislation for state and local governments. Over the past six years the Conference has been instrumental in an extensive record of innovative state action on problems of farmland preservation, pension fund investment, energy conservation, pay equity and comparable worth, environmental protection, economic development, and many other issues.

Frequent regional and national conferences, a publications program of over 100 titles, numerous pieces of model legislation, an effective professional staff, a bimonthly magazine _Ways & Means_, and numerous other services make up the program of the Conference.

For more information about the Conference, a sample issue of _Ways & Means_ or our Publications Catalogue, please write to Lee Webb, Executive Director.

THE ISSUES OF 1982: A BRIEFING BOOK

Editors:	David Jones
	Lee Webb

Editorial Assistants:	Mark Bohannon	Becky Stone
	Mary Buckley	Nancy Ylvisaker
	Jeff Good	

Production Coordinator: George Lehman

ISBN 0-89788-068-4

Introduction

America's 50 states are now rapidly growing in importance, and their influence is likely to continue to increase throughout the 1980s.

President Reagan's "New Federalism" coupled with long-term political and social trends are thrusting America's states back onto the center stage of American political life. For better or worse, decisions that used to be made in the commmittee rooms of Congress will be made increasingly in our 50 state legislatures.

This increased power of the states forces liberals and progressives to refocus their attention and resources. Since the New Deal, they have believed that the federal government was the sole instrument of social change in America. Their ideas, their lobbying and advocacy, their careers and their dreams focused on what Congress, the President, the regulatory agencies and the federal courts should do. State and local governments' potential and powers to confront the basic problems were ignored.

Moreover, massive cutbacks in federal aid to states, record unemployment and interest rates, and the transfer of responsibilities from Washington to the states are forcing the states to face issues they have ignored. In the past states were content with a limited portfolio of issues like highway construction, railroad and utility regulation and supervision of public schools. But now and increasingly the states are being expected to solve problems like rising health costs, air and water pollution, energy planning, tax equity, high interest rates, discrimination, child care, and even now the control of nuclear weapons.

The year 1982 will be a year of decision and opportunity. Will the states move squarely to confront the big problems faced by Americans, or will they turn their backs, claiming that they are "powerless" to act? Many of these issues are being fought now as states grapple with the effects of the massive cutbacks in federal aid, with the weakening or elimination of many federal regulatory programs, and the nationwide recession.

The state elections in November 1982 will also help
decide the role that states play in the 1980s. A record
number of candidates are running, including hundreds with
an activist background or progressive viewpoint. A combination
of the recession and reapportionment will bring many new
faces to the 50 state legislatures.

The Issues of 1982: A Briefing Book was written and
prepared for this new generation of state leaders likely to
play critical roles in the 1980s. Many of them are state
legislators, others statewide officials such as governors and
attorneys general, others leaders of citizen or civic organizations, and still others candidates for state legislative
or statewide office.

The Issues of 1982 covers the full range of issues that
states will face in 1982, and beyond. Thirty-five separate
issues are grouped under 10 broad sections which include:
economic issues; consumer issues; human services, natural
resources and the environment; labor and work; civil and
human rights; crime; education; the governmental process;
and national issues.

Each of the 35 issues is covered in a five page briefing
paper. The first page presents basic facts and statistics on
the issue. Pages two and three describe the major problems,
controversies, and policy choices surrounding the issue, the
fourth page outlines a concrete program of state action, including legislation, and the final page describes organizations
and publications that can be additional resources.

The individuals who contributed to this book by writing
individual briefing papers are some of the most intelligent
and brightest people in the country. Their knowledge of
their issues, their experience in policy analysis, and their
understanding of what states can do about the issues makes
this book a unique and extraordinary resource. Their
willingness to commit the time and energy to prepare these
remarkable papers is enormously appreciated.

The Issues of 1982: A Briefing Book is only one of the many resources available to state and local public officials, candidates, citizens and civic leaders from the Conference on Alternative State and Local Policies In addition to our bimonthly magazine Ways and Means, the Conference writes and publishes numerous reports, studies, monographs and handbooks. A full list of over 100 titles written and published by the Conference is available through our Publications Catalogue.

The year 1982 is an important year for America. Out of the legislative battles and the November elections can emerge a new generation of leaders in America's 50 states. We hope that The Issues of 1982 will play an important role in that process.

Lee Webb
Executive Director

Table of Contents

Economic Issues

Banking

BACKGROUND FACTS

The American economy is more nationally and globally interdependent than ever before. Capital flows further, faster, and with less public accountability than ever before.

States and communities are increasingly vulnerable to these flows of capital. New financial institutions are soaking up deposits in a state and are exporting them as loans to other states or even to other countries. Disinvestment -- originally a neighborhood problem -- is now a state and regional problem.

New money market funds are a big part of the problem. According to Angelo Bianchi of the Conference of State Bank Supervisors, "Money market mutual funds are bleeding numerous state and local communities of their economic life blood." Money market mutual funds' "massive shifts of assets have jeopardized the ability of many financial institutions to meet the investment and credit needs of their communities."

On interstate banking: "I don't think removing the barriers (from) Citibank is going to help me in my state. All they are going to do is take money out of my state and invest it in Eurodollars or in Zaire or maybe even in Iran," according to Bianchi.

The American banking industry is undergoing massive changes. The savings and loan industry is collapsing. Community banks are failing at an increasing rate. Banks are being consolidated and merged at an increasing rate. Banks and financial institutions are being deregulated. The federal government is preempting state banking regulation and laws. Banking is moving across state lines. Non-banks are moving into banking. And new technologies, especially automatic teller machines, promise major changes. All of these developments weaken states' ability to act on credit and banking issues.

The loss of state control over credit cost and availability comes at a time when states' credit needs are intensified by the shift of public responsibility for economic problems from the federal to the state level and to the private sector.

Federal program cutbacks, coupled with federally-induced erosion of the state tax base and rising state unemployment costs require states to expand control of public and private debt financing mechanisms to meet fundamental social and economic development objectives.

<u>THE PROBLEM</u>

The role of the states in regulating banking is being foreclosed at an ever accelerating pace. The nation's dual banking system, under which the state and federal governments enjoyed competitive equality in chartering and regulating financial institutions for the past hundred years, is rapidly coming to an end. If states are to protect and enhance their economic and social interests, a great deal of creativity will be needed over the next few years to shape the changing banking system to meet tomorrow's credit needs.

The cost and availability of debt capital to finance public, private and consumer needs are being determined increasingly in the board rooms of nationwide banking entities and the offices of the federal banking regulators. The ability of state legislatures to insure the availability and affordability of credit for housing, agriculture, industrial and commercial development, and consumer purchases through the banking industry is being steadily diminished.

The savings and loan industry is in crisis. Savings and loan associations are failing at a hectic pace. Over 80% experienced losses in 1981. Last year the Federal Savings and Loan Insurance Corporation forced 75 mergers involving over 150 savings and loans. Savings and loans have been merged across state lines and into commercial bank holding commpanies. Those savings and loans that survive are likely to be indistinguishable from commercial banks.

Since, proportionally, state chartered institutions tend 'to be smaller and the smaller institutions are failing more rapidly, the states' role will diminish in the years ahead.

The U. S. Congress and the federal regulators are preempting state banking law and regulation. Federal law eliminated state controls on interest rates (though the states can override this). The Federal Reserve Board now sets reserve requirements for all financial institutions, including state chartered banks and savings and loans. The Supreme Court has ruled the Federal Home Loan Bank Board's regulation permitting federal savings and loans to enforce the due-on-sale clause in mortgages is superior to state law.

Congress will likely enact major banking legislation in the near future which will further deregulate the banking industry. Where state law is not directly preempted, de facto preemption is likely because state chartered lenders will convert to federal charters if the states don't similarly deregulate.

The growth of nationwide banking will also undermine
state regulation. Financial institutions in over 30 states are
currently participating in multi-state automatic teller machine
(ATM) networks. Negotiations are underway to form nationwide
ATM networks, according to Business Week. The banking industry
and federal regulators are lobbying hard to eliminate federal
prohibitions on interstate banking -- an outcome that appears
inevitable.

In addition, the emergence of non-regulated banking entities
(for example, money market mutual funds, Sears, Merrill Lynch,
National Steel Corporation and Baldwin Pianos) pose great
problems for states since these corporations operate across
state lines with neither state or federal regulation.

The money market mutual funds and other recent entrants
into the financing industry operate with significant competitive
advantages because Congress and federal regulators have chosen
not to regulate them.

Because the changes in the banking industry are so radical
and being made so swiftly, policy responses have by and large
been piecemeal and incidental.

At the federal level, the Community Reinvestment Act (CRA)
has been the most significant response. The CRA imposed on
banks and savings and loans the responsibility for meeting
credit needs in local service areas, the areas from which the
deposits were taken. Although CRA isn't particularly specific
and has not been vigorously enforced, it has been a valuable
tool in improving credit availability in neighborhoods and
towns in many states. Numerous states have implemented community
reinvestment legislation or regulations.

Another state response has been to create alternative
financing vehicles to meet credit needs within the states. At
least 35 states have used housing finance agencies and mortgage
revenue bonds to meet particular housing credit needs. Commercial
revitalization, plant expansions and new factories have been
financed by industrial revenue bonds in many states. Some
states (Massachusetts being a prime example) have established
state agencies with bonding authority to finance economic
develoment. California has recently set up an Alternative
Energy System Financing Authority to provide credit for
renewable energy systems development.

States such as California have been actively seeking ways
to employ public pension funds to achieve state economic and
social objectives. Illinois is currently considering legislation
to facilitate more effective uses of public pension funds.

<u>WHAT STATES CAN DO</u>

<u>Redirect Banking Law</u>

° States should enact state Community Reinvestment Acts requiring financial institutions to help meet the credit needs of their local communities. California, Massachusetts, Ohio and other states have such laws and regulations.

° States should establish linked deposit programs under which deposits of state funds are placed with financial institutions committed to lending funds in ways that meet specified public policy objectives. Colorado and Illinois have such programs.

° States that permit out-of-state banks to establish banking facilities should pass legislation to ensure that the out-of-state banks meet the credit needs within the state.

<u>Alternative Credit Providing Institutions</u>

° States should establish a state-owned public bank and enable the establishment of municipally-owned banks. A public bank, like the Bank of North Dakota can help insure that the state's credit needs are being met.

° States should establish development finance agencies with authority to raise capital through issuing bonds. Thirty-nine states now have housing finance agencies to help meet various housing credit needs.

° States should use public pension funds to help meet credit and investment needs. In addition to giving legislative direction to pension fund trustees, states should establish risk reduction mechanisms (such as loan guarantees) to facilitate investment in higher risk ventures and secondary market mechanisms to package smaller loans for sale to the funds.

° States should help capitalize development banks like the South Shore Bank of Chicago, which provides credit in an inner-city neighborhood to help meet unmet or undermet credit needs to facilitate community development.

<u>Pressure on Federal Government</u>

° States should lobby Congress to reassert control of the Federal Reserve Board (FRB). The FRB is a creature of Congress but operates independently.

<u>FOR FURTHER INFORMATION</u>

<u>Publications</u>

"CRA: A Tool for Attracting Private Financing of Neighborhood Revitalization", Woodstock Institute, Larry Swift, 1981,
free. Explains the Community Reinvestment Act and how it can
be used to stimulate revitalization.

<u>Strategic Investment: An Alternative for Public Funds</u>, 1980
Conference on Alternative State and Local Policies, $5.95.

<u>Evaluation of the Illinois Neighborhood Development Cor-
poration</u>. Summary Report. Dennis Marino, <u>et al</u>, 1982. Available soon from Woodstock Institute.

<u>Investment Targeting -- A Wisconsin Case Study</u>, Donald
Smart, <u>et al</u>, 1979, Wisconsin Center for Public Policy. Develops
a model for the investment of public pension funds to help meet
state economic development goals.

<u>Pension Funds and Economic Renewal</u>, Lawrence Litvak, 1981.
Conference on Alternative State and Local Policies, $14.95.

<u>Social Investments and the Law: The Case for Alternative
Investment</u>, 1980, Conference on Alternative State and Local
Policies, $6.95.

<u>Selective Deposits of Public Funds</u>, Leonard Rubinowitz,
1977, Woodstock Institute, $3.00. An analysis of state and
local programs which link deposits of public money to reinvestment activities of banks.

<u>Organizations</u>

CENTER FOR COMMUNITY CHANGE, Neighborhood Revitalization Project,
1000 Wisconsin Ave., N.W., Washington, D.C., Allen Fishbein,
Director. Research and technical assistance organization which
publishes periodic legislative alerts on banking and neighborhood
reinvestment issues.

CONFERENCE ON ALTERNATIVE STATE AND LOCAL POLICIES, 2000
Florida Ave., N.W., Washington, D.C., Lee Webb, Director.
Publishes studies on banking and public investment policy and
periodic updates on new state and local legislation.

WOODSTOCK INSTITUTE, 410 N. Michigan Ave., Chicago, IL, Larry
Swift, President. Research ;and technical assistance organization focusing on neighborhood reinvestment and banking issues.

Prepared by Larry Swift.

Community Economic Development

<u>BACKGROUND FACTS</u>

Many of America's communities are in trouble. Inner city neighborhoods, rural counties, old industrial cities, minority neighborhoods face spiralling and persistent unemployment, poor public services, collapsing infrastructure, and abandoned buildings and homes.

Deteriorating national economic conditions are certainly intensified by the problems of many American communities. The economic health and qualityof life in hundreds of American communities is at stake. Cutbacks in Federal assistance for economic development and for community economic development mean that American communities will have to move in new directions for hope and assistance.

Unemployment among black youths is in excess of 50 percent and in some areas 75 percent. The adult unemployment rate on the large Navajo reservation in the Southwest is around 70% and 75% for black males in Miami.

In the stricken city of Youngstown, Ohio, 1300 individuals applied for 50 minimum wage jobs at the Bob Evans Farm Sausage Restaurant; in Nashville, Tennessee, 40,000 individuals applied for 800 jobs at a Japanese electronics plant.

The American job market is undergoing a rapid and fundamental transition from labor-intensive, heavy industry toward capital-intensive industries requiring trained, skilled professionals.

The restructuring of the American economy has had an enormous impact on communities dependent on heavy industry. Plant closings in these communities have caused slashes in public services and near-Depression levels of unemployment.

There is also a crisis developing in antiquated or nonexistent physical infrastructure, a necessity for economic growth. Roads, water systems, sewers, transportation lines, and physical plants are declining at a faster rate than they are being replaced.

Distressed communities also suffer from low business formation rates and high business failure rates. Business failure rate in distressed communities are in excess of 80%, due primarily to difficulty in obtaining conventional financing and lack of management experience.

<u>THE PROBLEM</u>

Community economic development is a process for revitalizing communities. It involves area residents in developing
comprehensive strategies and initiating activities in cooperation with local government and the private sector to generate
increased economic activity. Since many of these communities
have limited financial resources it is necessary to use
outside financial resources -- for example, federal, state,
and private funds -- to spur long-term economic revitalization.

Even in the best of times, distressed communities suffer a
disproportionate share of the economic barriers to development.
The economic problems compounded by a lack of both ownership
opportunities and circulation of dollars in the local community
leads to disinvestment and decline.

Community problems are accentuated by the decline of
physical infrastructure -- not only in the Northeast and Midwest but throughout the country. Lack of planning, time delays,
and the exorbitant costs of physical infrastructure projects
delay or negate private economic development initiatives.

While federal community economic development efforts are
being drastically reduced as a result of the President's "New
Federalism" program, innovative state efforts for community
economic development are increasing. The first state community economic develoment program, the Community Development
Finance Corporation (CDFC) of Massachusetts, was established
five years ago to provide venture capital financing for small
businesses in distressed communities. Wisconsin, Florida,
Alaska, and California have since initiatied similar programs.
Many innovative programs originated as state efforts to diversify economic development policy. States moved from simply
"smokestack chasing" to more comprehensive development
strategies emphasizing job creation through small business
activities -- the major sector of the economy with a demonstrated ability to create new jobs.

Profound world economic forces, labor and capital market
barriers, and federal policies constrain the ability of any
state or community to improve its own economy. Obviously,
some communities would not be experiencing severe underdevelop-
ment problems (unemployment, poor physical infrastructure,
and high business failure rate) if there were not significant
economic barriers to development. These barriers include lack
of information for judging sound business opportunities; the
cost of preparing and obtaining financing for businesses; risk
aversion of lending institutions; lack of training for current
and future jobs; and limited placement efforts for job openings.

Many conservatives argue that economic development and growth activities belong only to the private sector, and that only the private sector creates new jobs. They fail to recognize that there are significant barriers to private sector development, such as declining infrastructure and high risk. In addition, distressed communities have a limited private sector that cannot effectively mobilize the capital, assistance and management expertise needed to address overwhelming problems and issues.

Community economic development programs are also criticized as being part of the "urban renewal" activities of the late 1960's. Critics argue that urban renewal and public development activites have exacerbated development problems and wasted considerable amounts of taxpayer dollars because they have not created employment and ownership opportunities for low-income residents. Yet community economic development is actually the opposite of large-scale inefficient urban renewal efforts. It is predicated upon the involvement of local residents and the targeting of scarce development resources for small-scale projects with long-term impacts.

Both conservatives and progressives have viewed some government-funded community economic develement efforts as "pork barrel" programs. Critics argue that scarce federal and state dollars are used to finance projects in areas that are not distressed -- for example, that 85% of the U.S. population lives in areas eligible for Economic Development Administration (EDA) financing. Thus, some contend, community economic development programs are too costly, even if they have positive results.

Critics fail to recognize that community economic development reduces individual and community dependency and builds greater self-reliance within the communities. Increasing the dependency of a community, on the other hand, not only requires more public dollars, but also squanders valuable human resources. Community economic development, therefore, is often the most cost-effective way of revitalizing communities.

<u>WHAT STATES CAN DO</u>

<u>Community Economic Development Finance Programs</u>

° States should establish Community Development Finance Corporations (CDFCs). The Massachusetts legislature created
  such a corporation as a $10 million venture capital firm
  designed to finance business development in distressed
  communities.

° States should establish Community Development Finance Author-
  ities. Wisconsin signed into law on May 6, 1982, a bill
  creating a state community development finance authority.

° States should establish applicable loan programs to provide
  start-up costs to CDCs, such as the Florida Department of
  Community Affairs which provides low-interest loans on a
  competitive basis to business and physical development
  projects submitted by CDCs.

<u>Technical Assistance and Administrative Support</u>

° States should establish centers to provide technical assistance to new and expanding small businesses. The Community
  Economic Develoment and Assistance Center (CEDAC) is a
  sister corporation to CDFC in Massachusetts.

° States should establish grant programs to provide administrative support. The Florida Department of Community
  Affairs provides administrative grants of up to $100,000
  to between 10 to 20 urban and rural CDCs

<u>Other State Develoment Programs That Can Enhance Community</u>
<u>Economic Development</u>

° States should provide tax credits for contributions made
  to neighborhood assistance projects or commercial improvements projects. Seven states (Pennsylvania, Missouri, Indiana,
  Michigan, Delaware, Virginia, and Florida) have NAP programs.

° States should establish corporations that encourage capital
  investment in small, growth-oriented firms. Both Connecticut
  Project Development Corporation (CPDC) and the Indiana Corporation for Innovative Development (ICID) encourage capital
  investment in small, growth-oriented firms that cannot
  obtain conventional financing.

<u>FOR FURTHER INFORMATION</u>

<u>PUBLICATIONS</u>

<u>Community Development Corporations and State Development
Policy: Potential Partnerships</u>, Benson Roberts, Robert Zdenek,
and William Bivens. National Congress for Community Economic
Development, $15.00. Explores how CDCs and state governments
can develop innovative development and job creation programs.

<u>State Development Policy Series</u>. The Council of State
Planning Agencies, 400 N. Capitol St., N.W., Washington, D.C.,
20001. A series of monographs by experts in economic development issues such as pension funds, tax policy, development
finance, job creation, and physical infrastructure.

<u>Expanding the Opportunity to Produce</u>: Revitalizing the
<u>American Economy Through New Enterprise Development</u> edited
by Robert Friedman and William Schweke, $20.00 from the
Conference on Alternative State and Local Policies. A compila-
tion of articles discussing innovative strategies for economic
revitalization.

<u>ORGANIZATIONS</u>

CORPORATION FOR ENTERPRISE DEVELOPMENT, 2420 K St., N.W.,
Washington, D.C., 20037, (202) 298-8771, Robert Friedman,
President. Publishes books on enterprise development, and a
newsletter, The <u>Entrepreneurial Economy</u>.

COUNSEL FOR COMMUNITY DEVELOPMENT, INC., 10 Concord Ave.,
Cambridge, MA, 02138, (617) 492-5461, Belden Daniels, President.
Specializes in policy research and studies in economic develoment.
Extensive policy research at the state level resulting in the
creation of several state development finance institutions.

NATIONAL CONGRESS FOR COMMUNITY ECONOMIC DEVELOPMENT, 2025 Eye
St., N.W., #901, Washington, D.C. 20006, (202) 659-8411, Robert
Zdenek, President. A membership association of community-based
develoment organizations that publishes two monthly newsletters,
<u>Developments</u> and <u>Informer</u>; training through its affiliate the
National Training Institute for Community Economic Development
(NTICED);

NATIONAL ECONOMIC DEVELOPMENT AND LAW CENTER, 2150 Shattuck
Ave., Berkeley, CA, 94704, (415) 548-2460, David Kirkpatrick,
Vice President. Provides extensive technical assistance in
business packaging, legal and organizational issues.

Prepared by Robert Zdenek

Industrial Innovation

<u>BACKGROUND FACTS</u>

The root cause of most problems afflicting states today -- from declining budgets to high unemployment to plant closings to rising crime -- is our declining investment in industrial innovation and productivity.

For oft-discussed reasons -- rising resource and energy prices, tough international competition, poor corporate management, the export of capital abroad, increased military spending -- American businesses have been investing less in new product and process innovation than ever before. Symptoms of this decline include:

° <u>A lower productivity growth rate</u>. Manufacturing productivity has dropped from a 3.2% growth rate from 1948-65, to a 2.4% increase from 1965-73, to a 1.8% growth rate from 1973-78, to a 0.8% <u>drop</u> from 1978-80.

° <u>Declining international competitiveness</u>. Between 1973 and 1979, the United States ranked <u>10th</u> in productivity improvement among international competitors. Our overall productivity growth of 0.9% during this period lagged behind Sweden (1.8%), Italy (2.4%), Canada (2.5%), Japan (3.8%), Denmark (4.1%), Netherlands (4.2%), France (4.8%), Belgium (4.9%) and West Germany (5.0%).

° <u>Declining growth in real income</u>. Median family income grew at a 37.6% real average rate from 1950-59, 33.9% from 1960 to 1969, 6.7 % from 1970-79, and actually <u>declined</u> 5.5% in 1980.

Economists generally agree that American business has experienced a precipitous decline in the amount of funds invested in product and process innovation, successful technologies, and long-term product development. Only 35% of aggregate business non-residential investment today is devoted to new products and process, down from 75-80% in the 1950's and 1960's, according to Data Resources, Inc.

<u>THE PROBLEM</u>

The cause of our decreased investment in successful technologies and productivity improvements is poor use of capital,
not an aggregate "capital shortage."

Large, resource-dependent, established corporations and
businesses have a far stronger political voice than new, high
technology, relatively resource-efficient, growing industries.
As a result, many corporate and government decisions affecting
credit allocation during the past decade have been skewed towards wasteful uses of capital. Examples include:

° An enormous increase in capital devoted to new mergers and
  acquisitions, rather than productive investment in new
  technologies and processes. Mergers and acquisitions soaked
  up $82 billion in 1981 alone, up from $44 billion in 1980.

° Major misallocations of capital by large auto and steel companies. General Motors, Ford and Chrysler have consistently
  misjudged their markets, allowing the Japanese to earn 20%
  market-share. U.S. Steel has used its capital to diversify
  out of the steel industry -- most spectacularly in its bid
  for Marathon Oil -- rather than making the same investments
  in new product and process technology as their Japanese
  competitors.

° Increased military spending, which has not only diverted
  large amounts of investment capital away from badly needed
  innovation in our civilian industries, but, more importantly,
  has diverted research and development funds and top engineers.

° Deregulation of oil and natural gas prices, leading to the
  diversion of hundreds of billions of dollars from the
  general civilian economy to the treasuries of major oil
  and natural gas companies. These firms have tended to
  invest this capital in further resource exploitation, with
  which they are familiar, rather than in the unfamiliar --
  new and growing high technology sectors.

° Misguided tax policies, ranging from continuing tax breaks
  for the synthetic fuel, nuclear power, oil and gas industries,
  to the recent accelerated tax depreciation and "safe harbor"
  tax leasing schemes.

The Reagan Administration's "Accelerated Cost Recovery
System" (ACRS) gives increased tax benefits for investment
in industrial real estate, and actually <u>decreases</u> benefits
for the short-lived equipment used by most high technology
firms. "Safe harbor" leasing was specifically designed to
aid older firms, and is of little benefit to growing industries.

Current national policies have greatly exacerbated these problems. Burgeoning deficits leading to high interest rates have produced a "corporate liquidity crisis" unprecedented since the Depression. Business today is spending virtually all of its money to service short-term debt, pay salaries, replace vital equipment, and meet other day-to-day needs. Short-term debt service has skyrocketed; nearly half of U.S. corporate cash currently is being used just to pay off existing loans.

One key to restoring economic health, raising employment, and increasing living standards is to develop policies that increase our investment in industrial innovation and productivity.

Present policies encouraging nonproductive capital and credit allocation need to be changed. New policies are needed to encourage <u>productive</u> investment:

° <u>Eliminate policies encouraging unproductive investment.</u>
  We need to reduce unproductive military spending; use the Credit Control Act to discourage mergers and acquisitions; and eliminate tax breaks to the synthetic fuel, nuclear power, oil, natural gas and other older industries, focusing on drastically revising the ACRS act and eliminating the "safe harbor" leasing breaks.

° <u>Promote policies encouraging productive activity</u>. We need to encourage research and development into new, civilian sector, product and process developments; support education and job-training programs designed to equip workers for the new technological economy; support export promotion as an alternative to restricting free trade; and encourage programs designed to give employees a greater say and ownership in the firms within which they work.

° <u>Promote policies targeted to key sectors</u>. We need to target capital and other benefits to certain key sectors, particularly those targeted for development by strong international competitors like Japan, France and West Germany. For example, we need support for tax policies to aid semiconductor, computer, biotechnology, and other key high technology sectors which have become the driving force of our economic growth. Where tax policies are insufficent to guarantee economic health, we must consider a more direct government role in providing low-cost capital -- for example, through a national "Innovation Finance Corporation."

<u>WHAT STATES CAN DO</u>

<u>Promote Productive Investment of Pension and Tax Monies</u>

° States should enact legislation creating state venture
  capital corporations similar to the Connecticut New Product
  Development Corporation to make equity investments in new
  high technology companies that will expand the state's
  jobs.

° States should eliminate barriers preventing their public
  and private pension funds from investing some of their
  capital in high technology growth firms.

° States should promote tax policies designed to encourage
  productive investment, such as a recent California law
  eliminating the capital gains tax dividends paid by smaller
  firms, and making up the revenue loss by increasing taxes
  on gold, paintings and other collectibles.

<u>Promote Research and Development</u>

° States should set up joint research programs between industry
  and universities, as California has done with its MICRO
  project at the University of California. The project
  provides joint 1-1 matching grants for research and development projects in microelectronics and computer research.

<u>Promote Technological Literacy and High Technology Job Training</u>

° States should develop policies which emphasize equipping
  young people and older workers with the skills they need
  to survive in today's technological workplace. California
  has recently passed a $26 million "Investment in People"
  program, which funds teacher training and retraining in
  math, science and computer studies; high technology, employ-
  ment-based job training at the community colleges; increased
  support for engineering and computer science faculty at
  universities; and high technology training in existing
  apprenticeship programs.

<u>FOR FURTHER INFORMATION</u>

<u>Publications</u>

<u>Expanding the Opportunity to Produce: Revitalizing the American Economy Through New Enterprise Development</u>, edited by Robert Friedman and William Schweke, Corporation for Enterprise Development, 1981. Available for $19.95 from the Conference on Alternative State and Local Policies.

<u>State Policy Options for High Technology Promotion</u>, Governor's Office of Policy and Planning, State House, Trenton, NJ 08625.

<u>Organizations</u>

THE NATIONAL GOVERNORS ASSOCIATION TASKFORCE ON TECHNOLOGICAL INNOVATION, staff, Charlyn Cowan, NGA, 444 N. Capitol St., N.W. Washington, D.C. 20001. The NGA Taskforce on Technological Innovation, chaired by Governor Brown (CA) and Governor Milliken (MI) has compiled a booklet listing major state efforts around the nation to promote industrial innovation.

THE OFFICE OF ECONOMIC POLICY, PLANNING AND RESEARCH, of the Department of Economic and Business Development, State of California, Michael Kieschnick, 425 California St., Suite 701, San Francisco, CA, 94104 (415) 557-3020, is one of the best informed sources in the nation on state (and federal level) efforts to promote industrial innovation.

THE PUBLIC INVESTMENT UNIT, GOVERNOR'S OFFICE OF PLANNING AND RESEARCH, Nathan Gardels, 1400 10th St., Sacramento, CA, 95814 (916) 323-9563, is the nation's leading authority on state policies to promote productive investment by public and private pension funds.

NEW YORK OFFICE OF POLICY DEVELOPMENT, Office of the Governor, State Capitol, Albany, NY 12224.

THE CALIFORNIA COMMISSION ON INDUSTRIAL INNOVATION, Allison Thomas, Governor's Office, State Capitol, Sacramento, CA, 95814 (916) 324-0401, is a group of top California business, labor, academic and government leaders.

THE CALIFORNIA WORKSITE EDUCATION AND TRAINING ACT, Steve Dusche, 800 Capitol Mall, Sacramento, CA, 95814 (916) 323-3006, is an innovative job training program requiring an employment commitment to hire and substantial on-the-job training <u>prior</u> to funding training programs.

Prepared by Fred Branfman

Pension Fund Investment

BACKGROUND FACTS

Pension funds now have enormous influence in the American economy. Their influence will continue to grow rapidly.

The facts are staggering. Nationwide, pension funds have assets of over $650 billion. In 1980, public and private pension funds provided more that one-quarter of all new capital available for investment. It is estimated that by the end of the 1990's, pension funds will supply more than one-half the capital available for new investment.

Pension funds are major owners of American business. They own 25% of all publicly traded stock and 40% of all corporate bonds. To take just one example, the California Public Employees' Retirement System is the second largest stockholder in the Bank of America, fifth largest stockholder in Chase Manhattan Bank, and sixth largest in ARCO.

Almost all of the stock pension funds own is concentrated in the country's largest 500 corporations. State legislation now governing public pension funds virtually restricts equity investment to these firms.

Pension funds have tremendous potential over corporate management through the voting rights attached to stock ownership. Up to now there has been a tendency to vote with corporate management on stockholder issues -- especially on the part of pension funds managed by banks. (At the end of 1975, the 100 largest banks controlled over $145.6 billion in pension funds.)

Pension funds are deferred wages, the collective retirement savings of workers. Until recently, workers and retirees belonging to retirement plans showed little interest in how their pension funds were managed or invested. This is changing. Many unions are now actively interested in how their pension funds are invested. Some union funds have withdrawn their investments from non-union companies; others have used the threat of divestiture to help with organizing campaigns. The AFL-CIO leadership has called for union participation in pension fund management to aid in revitalizing the economy.

Public pension funds provide opportunities for investing on behalf of the public account, and especially for targeting investment to a state's economic development needs.

<u>THE PROBLEM</u>

Public pension funds, which depend for their health on a strong economy, have a self-interest in promoting jobs and economic development in their own states. Many private pension plans have a similar interest when contributions to the funds are derived primarily from the local economy.

Most pension funds, however, are invested without regard for the impact of the investment on the state or local economy, or on the interests of the beneficiaries.

Looked at another way, public employee and private pension funds are the largest capital resource available in any state. The challenge is to match this resource with states' capital needs. Increasing the flow of pension capital into productive investment, thereby creating more employment opportunities, one might allow states to reduce their budget expenditures for welfare and unemployment. Increasing the tax base in this way will support the ability of states and localities to adequately fund their retirement systems.

Pension fund managers have long argued that they can produce the best returns when they have complete freedom to invest. More and more members of retirement systems, however, are challenging this axiom. Throughout the 1970's, in fact, investment in mortgages for members would have produced a better return for pension funds than their investments in stocks and bonds -- while also providing immediate benefit to plan members, and at no greater risk.

In a nutshell: development investing -- investing with regard for the interests of beneficiaries and of the state and local economy -- can offer financial returns equal to or greater than traditional pension fund investment policy. Development investing, however, is opposed by many fund managers and by many pension plan trustees.

Most public pension funds are governed by legislation specifiying how they can be invested. These statutory restrictions strongly favor investment in the stocks and bonds of the largest corporations. The restrictions sometimes state what portion of the total portfolio is to be invested in stocks, and what portion in bonds. Some public funds are restricted from investment in real estate altogether. Where this is the case, development investing will have to wait on changes in the legislation.

The composition of the trustee body charged with fiduciary responsibility for the pension fund greatly influences investment policy. Some pension funds exclude members or beneficiaries from representation on the board of trustees, thus allowing

members no say whatsoever in investment or fund management
decisions. Some pension funds are managed entirely by bank
trust departments. Alteration of the trustees' authority or
composition of the board of trustees requires legislative
changes.

The trustees of most pension funds -- who are dispropor-
tionately bankers and representatives of large business interests
-- are conservative, and with good reason: the responsibility
of guaranteeing the safety of retirement funds for hundreds or
thousands of workers is an awesome one. Still, many trustees
are threatened by the new interest members and their unions
are taking in the investment and management of pension funds.

The Employee Retirement Income Security Act (ERISA) of
1974, the federal legislation regulating private pension
funds, charges trustees with maximizing the return of their
funds consistent with the "prudent expert" rule (i.e., investments must be those which would be made by a prudent person
acting in a like capacity). Department of Labor interpreta-
tions of ERISA have encouraged trustees to pursue conservative
investment strategies.

Many trustees feel that investments targeted to job
creation, local economic development, housing, or mortgages for
members present unacceptable levels of risk for a pension fund.
The lack of a long track record for alternative investments by
pension funds further increases the risk factor, some fund
managers believe.

Everyone active in the pension fund arena -- plan members
and beneficiaries, union, trustees, advisors -- agree that
prudence has to be the basis of all investment decisions so
that retirement income can be secure. The financial integrity
of a retirement system must be the cardinal concern of any
pension investment policy

<u>WHAT STATES CAN DO</u>

<u>Mandate Employee Involvement in Decision-Making</u>

° State should enact legislation requiring that state and local
  pension funds have public employees and retirees represented
  on the fund's board of trustees or investment committee.

° States should enact legislation requiring the disclosure of
  financial information and investment information to public
  employees and retirees.

° States should enact legislation giving public employees a
  strong voice in voting shares held by the pension fund on
  corporate proxy issues. States could also require a pension
  fund to submit a proxy resolution if, for example, 10 percent of the system's participants request it.

<u>Create an Agency to Make New Investments</u>

° States should create State Commissions or Task Forces to
  analyze the investment policies of their public employee pension funds and recommend new "dynamic" investment policies
  for the fund. In addition, states could create a Pension
  Fund Investment Unit to assist state and local funds in
  making innovative investments.

<u>Investing in Housing</u>

° States should enact legislation requiring that public
  pension funds invest in mortgages for public employees.

° States should enact legislation requiring pension funds to
  invest a certain percentage of their assests in low- and
  middle-income housing.

<u>Business and Economic Development</u>

° States should enact legislation allowing pension fund trustees
  greater latitude in investing in smaller, high technology
  corporations.

° States should enact legislation allowing a small percentage
  of the funds assets to be invested in venture capital businesses.

<u>Responsible Investing</u>

° States should enact legislation requiring that pension fund
   trustees consider "social responsibility criteria" such as a
   firm's fair labor practices, affirmative action, environmental
   protection, product quality before investing in a particular
   firm's stocks or bonds.

<u>FOR FURTHER INFORMATION</u>

<u>Publications</u>

    <u>Studies in Pension Fund Investment</u>, Conference on Alter-
native State and Local Policies, 2000 Florida Avenue, N.W.,
Washington, D.C., 20009. A series of reports on pension fund
policy and state and local experiences with alternative pension
fund investment.

    <u>The North Will Rise Again: Pensions, Politics and Power
in the 1980s</u>, Randy Barber and Jeremy Rifkin, Beacon Press
paperback, 1978. The most influential book on this issue to
date, especially the labor movement.

    <u>A Model Agenda for State and Local Governments: Public
Pension Fund Investment</u>, William Schweke. Legislative Brief
82-12-EC-1. Washington, D.C.: Conference on Alternative State
and Local Policies, 1982.

    <u>Pension Funds and Economic Renewal</u>, Lawrence Litvak,
Council of State Planning Agencies, 1981.

    <u>Alternative Investing by State and Local Pension Funds:
Survey of Current Practices</u>, John Petersen and Catharine Spain,
Government Finance Research Center, Municipal Finance Officers'
Association, 1980.

    <u>Final Report</u> of the Governor's Public Investment Task Force,
October 1981. Available from the Pension Investment Unit,
Governor's Office of Planning and Research, 1400 Tenth Street,
Room 206, Sacramento, CA.

<u>Organizations</u>

CONFERENCE ON ALTERNATIVE STATE AND LOCAL POLICIES, 2000
Florida Avenue, N.W., Washington, D.C., 20009, (202) 387-6030.
Have published a 13 volume series of books on innovative pension
fund investing.

INVESTOR RESPONSIBILITY RESEARCH CENTER, 1319 F Street, N.W.,
Washington, D.C., (202) 803-3728. An information service for
investors, on stockholder resolutions presented to corporations
and on corporate response to social issues.

PEOPLES BUSINESS COMMISSION, 1346 Connecticut Avenue, N.W.,
Washington, D.C., 20009, (202) 466-2823, Randy Barber.

PENSION INVESTMENT UNIT, Governor's Office of Planning and
Research, 1400 Tenth Street, Room 206, Sacramento, CA, 95814,
(916) 323-9563, Nathan Gardels, Director.

Prepared by David Olsen.

Plant Closings

Most states are confronted by the spectre of plant closings. Between 1969 and 1976, an estimated 15 million Americans were thrown out of work because of plant closures.

There are many reasons for plant closings, such as reduced demand for production and corporate investment decisions resting upon considerations of labor, transportation and energy costs. Moreover, federal laws actually encourage plant closings through tax breaks.

Plant closings usually have critical repercussions. A northeastern manufacturer may, over time, close down several facilities and shift operations to Taiwan, throwing thousands of employees out of work. When a company closes a factory, businesses servicing the employees are forced to cut back, aggravating area unemployment. Unemployed workers may spend months or years finding new jobs.

At worst, plant closings reak havoc on individual lives, such as when eight former workers at the Federal Mogul Plant in Detroit committed suicide following the plant's closing.

The heavily industrialized areas of the Northeast and Midwest have suffered most from plant closures and the flight of capital and assets to other locations. From 1969 to 1976, corporations in the "Frostbelt" states (Connecticut, Massachusetts, Michigan, Minnesota, Missouri, New York, Pennsylvania and Ohio) eliminated 111 jobs through plant shutdowns for every 100 new jobs they created. Business Week noted in 1976 that "Capital from the Northeast and Midwest has financed the industrial expansion of the South."

But southern states have also felt the impact of plant closures -- in fact, the rate of manufacturing plant closures is higher in the South than in any other region of the country.

Plant closings are now hitting such previously untouched areas as California and the Pacific Northwest states.

Where are the corporations going? To a great extent, overseas -- where labor costs are often lower. American corporate overseas investment rose tenfold from an estimated $11.8 billion in 1950 to $118.6 billion in 1974.

<u>THE PROBLEM</u>

When a manufacturing operation shuts down, it creates a chain of problems for displaced workers, local communities and state governments. Plant closings hit hardest at industrial workers with seniority who have difficulty starting their careers over again. These workers may spend months or years searching for new employment --though their unemployment benefits may run out long before they find work.

The ripple effects of plant closings on local communities and states can be equally devastating. These effects include: shattered tax bases; strains on government resources, as many of the unemployed are forced to seek public assistance; lost revenues to local businesses as residents' purchasing power shrinks; and what one observer calls "an industrial 'refugee' crisis of substantial magnitude--whole subcommunities without jobs."

Plant closings are caused by "capital flight." This capital mobility does not always translate into the actual shutting down of a facility and relocating its operations. It can also mean: 1) gradually shifting equipment, employees or corporate activities from one location to another--keeping the original facility operating but at less capacity 2) running down older facilities and investing the savings elsewhere 3) "milking" older facilities--that is, using profits from them to bolster other corporate activities.

Capital mobility itself cannot be stopped. As plant closings experts Barry Bluestone, Bennett Harrison and Lawrence Baker note, "In a world of growing material scarcity, resources must be allocated in a wise and thoughtful mannner." According to the writers, "The basic issue, then, is not how to stop capital movement. It is instead how to assure that this trans fer of capital from one use or location to another will meet real human needs without disregarding the full impact of such decisions on people and their communities."

Maine, Michigan and Wisconsin have laws affecting plant closings. In Maine, companies with 100 or more employees which intend to shut down operations must give workers employed three or more years one week of severance pay for each year of employment. The law provides for civil damages for noncompliance.

Michigan recently enacted the first state law for financing employee ownership, including buyouts of closing plants. The newly-created Economic Development Authority is required to finance at least five industrial conversion projects each year.

Wisconsin is the only state requiring companies to give notice (sixty days) of impending shutdowns. Failure to give such notice can lead to fines of up to $50 per affected employee.

Twenty-one other states are currently considering plant closing legislation. Passage, however, will be difficult because of intense business lobbying.

Corporations make two major arguments against state plant closing legislation: 1)that companies will refuse to locate in states with plant closings laws, and 2)that expansion of service sector employment will more than compensate for the manufacturing jobs lost through plant closings.

Though corporations loudly protest when state governments consider legislation to mitigate the effects of plant closings, many of these same businesses have learned to operate success-fully in countries such as Great Britain and West Germany, which have strict plant closure laws.

Plant closing laws have not kept business out of a state, corporate warnings notwithstanding. For example, United Tech-nologies Corporation, the parent company of Pratt and Witney Aircraft, testified against a Connecticut plant closings bill, warning it would never expand its business operations in the state if the legislation were passed. Yet a few months later, Pratt and Witney, after looking into more than 30 pos-sible locations in the eastern U.S. for a new plant, set up shop in Maine -- the only eastern state with a plant closings law and the means for enforcing it.

The argument that expansion of service employment more than compensates for the jobs lost from plant closings--and therefore, that plant closings are really not a serious problem--ignores both the nature of the service economy and the problems of those workers trained in manufacturing. Non-manufacturing jobs are frequently low-paying, are often part-time and are usually filled by young people with special training, not middle-aged displaced factory workers. An auto assembly line worker with ten years seniority will have great difficulty becoming a computer programmer--especially when no job retraining is available.

If states are to be spared the economic and human costs of plant closings, legislatures must enact laws requiring advance notice of shutdowns and establishing mechanisms for managing the transition period.

<u>WHAT STATES CAN DO</u>

<u>Prenotification</u>

° States should pass legislation requiring one year advance
  notice of intent to close or relocate a company or displace
  over 15% of the firm's employees. Prenotification is the
  critical factor that gives government and workers the time
  to prepare for layoffs and shutdowns and enables them to
  best use adjustment measures.

<u>To Assist Workers</u>

° States should create an Economic Adjustment Task Force for
  retraining workers, placing them in new jobs, modernizing
  business facilities and meeting workers' basic economic needs.

° States should set up programs for jobless workers to commute
  from counties affected by plant closures and mass layoffs
  to other communities. California is presently designing a
  program to match the skills of Salinas/Monterey area workers
  with job opportunities in the San Jose/Santa Clara area.

° States should instruct all public lenders, such as state
  housing finance agencies and veteran loan programs, to
  restructure payment arrangments for persons unemployed as
  a result of plant closings.

° States should provide health insurance benefits to unemployed and disabled individuals who are eligible for unemployment
  compensation payments.

<u>Employee Buyouts</u>

° States should create development banks that can finance
  employee buyouts. States could require recipients of the
  aid to set aside a minimum percentage of stock to be
  employee-owned. The Massachusetts Community Development
  Finance Corporation, for example, can make debt or equity
  investments in worker-owned businesses.

<u>Severance Payments</u>

° States should require the company to pay a sum equal to 15%
  of the total annual payroll into a Community Assistance
  Fund. Such a fund would be used to preserve current jobs,
  to attract new industry into the community or to maintain
  the existing tax base.

° States should pass legislation requiring the closing firm
  to make severance payments to the terminated employees equal
  to one week's pay for each year worked.

<u>FOR FURTHER INFORMATION</u>

<u>Publications</u>

    <u>Corporate Flight</u>, Barry Bluestone, Bennett Harrison and
Lawrence Baker, 1981. Available for $3.95 from the Conference
on Alternative State and Local Policies. A thorough examination
of the causes, consequences and responses to plant closings.

    <u>Plant Closings: Resources for Public Officials and Trade
Unionists</u>, Ed Kelly and Lee Webb, 1979. Available for $5.95
from the Conference on Alternative State and Local Policies.
A compendium of articles on plant closings, including European
policies, state initiatives and federal responses.

    <u>Plant Closings Briefing Book: Issues, Politics and Legi-
slation</u>, William Schweke, 1981. Available for $5.95 from
the Conference on Alternative State and Local Policies.
Compares state plant closings legislation, describes two
national bills to solve the problem and lists people and
organizations for additional information.

<u>Organizations</u>

CONFERENCE ON ALTERNATIVE STATE AND LOCAL POLICIES, 2000
Florida Ave., N.W., Washington, D.C. (202) 387-6030, Lee
Webb, Director. Publishes studies on plant closings and
periodic updates on new state legislation.

INDUSTRIAL COOPERATIVE ASSOCIATION, 2161 Massachusetts
Ave., Cambridge, MA 02140 (617) 542-4245. A technical assistance organization that works with employees and unions on
employee buy-outs.

NATIONAL CENTER FOR EMPLOYEE OWNERSHIP, 1611 Walter Reed
Drive, Room 109 Arlington, VA 22204 (703) 931-2757, Corey
Rosen, Executive Director. NCEO sells a variety of publications
explaining the legal, economic and organizational aspects of
employee ownership.

OHIO PUBLIC INTEREST CAMPAIGN, 340 Chester, 12th Building,
Cleveland, OH 44114 (216) 861-5200, Ed Kelley, Research
Director. A statewide citizens group focusing on plant
closings, energy and tax policy.

UNITED AUTO WORKERS, 8000 East Jefferson, Detroit, MI 48214
(313) 926-5000. Sheldon Friedman, Research Director. Friedman
is a leading specialist on the issue. The UAW has done
extensive research on the issue and has lobbied for state
and national plant closings legislation.

Prepared by David Jones and William Schweke.

Small Business

<u>BACKGROUND FACTS</u>

Approximately 98% of all businesses can be considered
"small." Only 10,000 of the nation's businesses have 500 or
more employees. Small business employs 47% of the non-govern-
mental labor force.

Almost 80% of all net new jobs come from firms with
fewer than 100 employees, according to research done at MIT
between 1969 and 1976, and two-thirds of all new jobs are
accounted for by firms with 20 or fewer employees. Futhermore,
in the Northeast small business also compensated for job
opportunities <u>lost</u> by the largest corporations during the
same period. National Science Foundation and Commerce Department reports concluded that small business was "24 times
more innovative per research and development dollar than
large firms." Thus, contrary to popular belief, a state's
job creation, even in the sunbelt states, will come from
fostering local businesses, not from attracting business
from out of state.

Yet for small business, lack of access to capital is a
major problem, and the general economic recession has severely
magnified this problem. According to Dunn and Bradstreet
(U.S. News and World Report, May 3, 1982) business failures
in the first fourteen weeks of 1982 were running 55% ahead of
the comparable period in 1981, and 2.5 times the comparable
period in 1980. If the 1982 levels continue, (and there is
every indication that they will), the failure rate will exceed
the levels reached in 1932.

Venture capital is important to growing small businesses,
but not as important as often assumed. In a $3 trillion
economy that invests over $500 billion a year in capital, the
venture capital industry accounts for approximately $1 billion
a year, or one fifth of one percent. That money is invested
in a few thousand of the ten to thirteen million small business
concerns in the United States.

By contrast, regulated financial institutions in the
United States, including banks, savings and loans, thrifts,
savings banks, credit unions, insurance reserves, and pension
funds control over five trillion dollars a year in assets.

Commercial banks alone control over $2 trillion in
assets. The average sized state has approximately $40 billion
in assets in commercial banks.

<u>THE PROBLEM</u>

Financial institutions are regulated at both the state and federal level, with the federal government dominating. The exception is that states regulate insurance reserves. Since the 1930s, regulatory policy has focused on assuring the safety and soundness of the institutions, with little thought given to how regulation affects the ability of these institutions to meet legitimate capital needs. (Housing has been an exception to this pattern.)

Ironically, this focus on safety and soundness - which usually takes the form of prohibiting institutions from taking any risk in their investment activity - may have contributed significantly to the economic malaise now eating away at the financial institutions themselves.

High interest rates are having a devastating impact on the ability of small businesses to survive and prosper. Most small businesses finance their working capital with short term, bank-financed debt. The gyrating increases in the interest rates have severely strained the debt-service capabilities of most small businesses. Without the internal reserves to withstand the long period of high rates, and without an ability to fully pass along these increased "costs" of doing business to their customers, small businesses are closing their doors in increasing numbers. The farm sector, comprised mostly of small businesses, has also experienced a steep economic decline.

Over the most recent business cycle, the cost of credit (interest rates) and the variability of these rates, rather than credit availability, have been the major problem because they undermine the ability of business managers to plan, profit flows are much less predictable, and the risks of undertaking new investments greater.

Since approximately 80% of small businesses rely on financing from depository institutions an increase in the cost of financing and a decrease in the availability of funds has a more severe impact on smaller firms then on larger firms. (President's Report, p. 122).

For potentially growing businesses, the problem of capital access is severe. Options are severely limited for businesses that cannot provide security, collateral or guarantees for loans from banks whose major management and regulatory responsibility is to avoid any risk. They must then turn to personal money, family and friends; utilization of non-business assets as collateral; or in rare cases private venture capital.

The Small Business Administration's direct loan and loan
guarantee programs have helped, but are being reduced. In
fact, the SBA program is a very modest capital correcting
mechanism that needs expansion to counter the government's
capital market interference.

There is some controversy over whether capital access is
the most important problem or whether the cost of capital is
more important. Both are important, but some capital access
problems can be solved through modest and inexpensive market
restructuring, while reducing the cost of capital is largely
a question of federal fiscal and monetary policy and/or
expensive subsidies. (It is interesting that the housing
lobby organized support for a $3 billion capital subsidy,
but no such suggestion is seriously pursued for productive
small businesses.) It is important to remember that the
suggestions being proposed are basically oriented toward
improving capital access, not reducing the capital cost.
This will help many businesses at little or no government
cost, but will not solve the problem for other businesses
that require capital to survive or expand.

These program proposals aim not exclusively to satisfy a
small business constituency, but to create a climate of
economic and job growth. The potential entrepreneur and the
struggling, growing company -- not mature small businesses
more interested in protecting their gains -- are targeted for
aid. The goal of making financial institutions more responsive
to the needs of small businesses will be well received, but
specific program proposals will extend beyond the interests
of the organized small business political constituencies.
Therefore, the ideas must be pursued as part of an overall
strategy of economic growth, not as a small business
constituency issue.

<u>WHAT STATES CAN DO</u>

<u>Bank Regulation</u>

° States should require financial regulators, in their annual
  report to the Governor and legislature, to report on the
  performance of the institutions in supporting productive
  business development.

° States should develop a state level equivalent of the 1977
  federal "community reinvestment act," which directed regulators to consider the needs of the community in their
  decisions. Such an act should focus on productive business
  investment rather than on housing or consumer loans.

° States should ensure that small businesses are represented
  on the boards of directors of major financial institutions.
  (Surprisingly, the major banks seldom have small business
  representation.)

<u>New State Programs</u>

° States should establish Loan Loss Reserve Programs. These
  programs develop a special reserve fund to allow banks to
  make loans of more than normal risk. They work best in states
  that have a substantial percentage of banking assets in large
  banks, since the program requires each participating bank
  to develop a loss reserve covering a broad portfolio of loans.

° States should create a new class of commercial lenders to
  provide funds for venture capital firms. California,
  Nevada and some other states have created "Business and
  Industrial Development Corporations" (BIDCOs) to generate
  more sophisticated financing for venture capital companies.
  (Some single company BIDCOs exist in other states but are
  not the same.) These institutions make government guaranteed
  loans and sell the guarantees to leverage their funds.
  Since they do not take deposits and do not have fiduciary
  responsibility or federal insurance, they can take equity
  positions and develop much more flexible financing responses
  than is the case for banks.

<u>Investing Pension Funds</u>

° States should use pension funds and insurance reserves for
  small business development. Investments in smaller businesses,
  after accounting for overhead and risk, can generate better
  returns than investments in larger companies. A strategy
  is needed to assure a more balanced investment portfolio
  for insurance reserves and pension funds.

<u>FOR FURTHER INFORMATION</u>

<u>Publications</u>

Banking and <u>Small Business</u>, 1981, Derek Hanson, Council
of State Planning Agencies, available for $14.95 from the
Conference on Alternative State and Local Policies.

<u>Expanding the Opportunity to Produce</u>, 1981, Robert
Friedman and Bill Schweke, eds. Corporation for Enterprise
Development. Collection of articles by 52 nationally prominent
experts on promoting new enterprise development. Available
for $19.95 from the Conference on Alternative State and
Local Policies.

<u>The Entrepreneurial Economy: A Monthly Review of
Enterprise Development Strategies</u>, available from the
Corporation for Enterprise Development, $19.95/year plus
$2.50 UPS. A recently launched monthly newsletter.

<u>Pension Funds and Economic Renewal</u>, 1981, Lawrence Litvak,
Council of State Planning Agencies. Available from the
Conference on Alternative State and Local Policies, $14.95.

<u>Small Business Policy for California</u>, California State
CETA Office, Attention: MATS Unit, 80 Capitol Mall, Mic 77,
Sacramento, CA, 95814.

<u>Small Business and State Economic Development</u>, available
through the Counsel for Community Development, Inc., 10
Concord Ave., Cambridge, MA.

<u>Organizations</u>

CONFERENCE ON ALTERNATIVE STATE AND LOCAL POLICIES, 2000
Florida Ave., N.W., Washington, D.C., 20009, (202) 387-6030.

CORPORATION FOR ENTERPRISE DEVELOPMENT, 2420 K St., N.W.,
Washington, D.C., 20037, (202) 298-8771.

COUNCIL OF STATE PLANNING AGENCIES, 444 North Capitol Street,
Suite 291, Washington, D.C., 20001, 202-624-5386.

NATIONAL FEDERATION OF INDEPENDENT BUSINESS, L'Enfant Plaza
East, SW, Washington, DC.

OFFICE OF POLICY DEVELOPMENT, Office of the Governor, State
Capitol, Albany, NY 12224.

Prepared by Derek Hansen.

Tax Reform

In seven of the eight years preceding Ronald Reagan's election to the Presidency, the net effect of state and local legislative actions on taxes was to reduce total tax collections.

This has changed. In 1981, states by themselves raised taxes by more than $4 billion. And it is likely that 1982 will see states add another $5 - $8 billion to their total tax bill. Cities and counties too have begun to raise property taxes, and have begun to charge new or higher fees for the provisions of various services, ranging from sewage treatment to library cards.

It is no accident that this sharp reversal of trend coincides with the onset of the Reagan economic program. That program has put severe pressure on the financial security of state and local governments, in four principal ways.

First, grants-in-aid to state and local governments have suffered more than their fair share of the Reagan budget cuts. Even though these grants made up only 14% of total federal spending, Reagan cuts will reduce aid to the states as a percentage of total federal spending to pre-Great Society levels.

Second, the recession, made more severe by Reagan's tax and spending policies, has caused dramatic reductions in tax collections and equally dramatic increases in claims on government services.

Third, the ill-named Economic Recovery Tax Act of 1981 (ERTA) contained a number of new tax-free investment vehicles. These tax giveaways have crowded-out the market for state and local bonds, driving up interest rates.

Fourth, the Accelerated Cost Recovery System (ACRS), which will reduce annual federal corporate income tax collections by 40% in 1986, will cause similar damage to state corporate tax revenues. Conformity to ACRS will result in a $27.5 billion loss to the states.

Given this context, states and cities have been forced to raise taxes -- and will continue to be forced to raise taxes. That much is clear. The only questions remaining to be resolved are "Which taxes?" and "Who will pay them?"

<u>THE PROBLEM</u>

The shift in funding responsibility away from the federal
government toward state and local governments means a shift
from a tax system based on a mildly progressive income tax to
tax systems based on regressive sales and property taxes.
But there are alternatives. Much can be done to restructure
state and local tax systems to make them less regressive.
In this way, both the fairness and the level of state and
local taxes can be increased.

There are two major obstacles to this effort:

1. A widespread belief that the level of state and local
   taxes is a key determinant of business location
   decisions, and

2. Insensitivity to the issue of tax fairness on the
   part of progressives, citizens groups, and labor
   organizations.

Business taxes are a critical element of any progressive
tax system. Without them, most income generated from the
ownership of capital, for example, stocks and bonds, would go
untaxed. (And since the richer a person is, the greater is
the proportion of his or her income that is "unearned," low
business taxes mean a significant reduction in the overall
tax burdens of the wealthy.)

This is only true, of course, if business taxes aren't
"passed through" to consumers. The fact that business lobbyists
become so enraged at the very mention of a business tax hike
suggests that businesses don't possess the kind of ability to
pass-through taxes that they often. So does the fact that
these same lobbyists never argue that lower business taxes
might result in <u>lower</u> consumer prices.

More specifically, though, the ability of businesses to
pass-through taxes is limited by the amount of competition
facing a particular business, and the number of substitutes
for the product produced by a particular business. The
greater the competition, and the larger the number of substitutes, the less the ability to "pass-through" taxes. Even
firms with substantial monopoly power will be limited in
their ability to pass-through taxes, since they will have
already pushed and probed the market to determine what price
maximizes profits. A tax increase won't change this price.

Therefore, the owners of businesses -- shareholders,
partners, and sole proprietors -- ultimately bear the lion's
share of the burden of business taxes. And only if this is
true does the "business tax climate" argument make any sense
at all.

Still, the notion that state and local taxes play a key
role in the location decisions of businesses cannot stand up
to scrutiny. State and local taxes make up ony 2 to 3% of a
business's total costs; interstate differences in the level
of these taxes constitute only a small fraction of this 2-3%.
Moreover, since state tax payments are deductible from federal
tax liability, whatever difference in tax levels exists between
states is automatically halved. Compared to interstate differences in labor or energy costs, interstate differences in the
cost of state and local taxes are insignificant.

However, firms look at more than just the costs of doing
business in different locations, they also look at the relative
benefits of different sites. Among those benefits are things
government provides -- good roads and bridges so that products
can be transported efficiently, good schools so that workers
are productive, good sewers, good police and fire protection,
and so on. If states and localities do not have enough money
to provide these services, then the relative attractiveness
of their state or their locality will be diminished. Thus,
by giving away their business tax bases, states and localities
which have bought into the "business tax climate" view, may
actually be losing their ability to provide those things
which really are key determinants of business locations.

Finally, the positive obligation of businesses to help
pay for government should be asserted. Justice Holmes once
remarked, "Taxes are the price we pay for a civilized society."
Certainly businesses are among the primary beneficiaries of
civilized society. Our court system protects the rights of
individuals to contract freely with one another, and protects
the inviolability of these contracts. Police and fire protection provide security from wanton attacks on private property.
Highways and bridges allow the transport of goods between
cities. Public schools provide the skilled labor force needed
to keep our country competitive in international markets.
In short, because businesses benefit from government services
they should help pay for them.

The progressive political movement has failed to take
seriously the issue of tax fairness for middle- and lower-
income taxpayers. Focusing their attention exclusively on
the expenditure side of federal, state, and local budgets,
progressives have permitted right-wing crusaders like Howard
Jarvis and Jack Kemp to dominate public debate on taxes.
Exploiting popular frustration with very real tax burdens,
these individuals have successfully promoted legislation
which has done very little to reduce the real tax burdens of
the veas majority of Americans, but have very significantly
slashed the taxes of the wealthiest individuals and corporations in this country.

WHAT STATES CAN DO

Business Taxation

° States should "decouple" from ACRS -- permanently. The
  simplest way to "decouple" from ACRS revenue loss is to
  require that businesses add-back for state income tax
  purposes a certain percentage of the ACRS deductions claimed
  at the federal level. This step will prevent the elimination
  of corporate income tax.

° States should adopt the "unitary-world wide combination"
  system of reporting corporate profits. This would require
  multi-state or multi-national corporations to report total
  worldwide profits, and pay taxes on the share proportionate
  to the state's interest.

° States should stop tax abatements designed to promote
  economic development, particularly in urban areas.

Income Taxation

° States should enact income taxes if they do not already
  have them. These should be graduated taxes.

° States should give their counties and cities the authority
  to enact graduated income taxes.

° States should exempt items from the sales tax such as
  food, clothing and prescription drugs which are major
  spending items for low- and moderate-income families.

Property Taxation

° States should enact property tax "circuit breakers," which
  reimburse individuals whose property taxes exceed a certain
  percentage of family income.

° States should enact metropolitan tax base sharing to allevi-
  ate property tax disparities between cities and their
  suburbs. Minnesota, for instance, has adopted a plan in
  which 40% of any industrial or commercial growth in certain
  metropolitan areas is shared by all the communities in
  that area.

Other

° States and localities should include "intangible" property
  such as stocks, bonds and other types of paper wealth
  in their property tax base.

<u>FOR FURTHER INFORMATION</u>

<u>Publications</u>

<u>Interstate Tax Competition</u>, Advisory Commission on
Intergovernmental Relations, Washington, D.C.: ACIR,
<u>Significant Features of Federalism, 1979-80</u>.

<u>How the States Can Respond to the 1981 Changes in Federal
Depreciation Rules</u>, 1981. Washington, D.C.: Citizens for Tax
Justice.

<u>The Shifting Property Tax Burden: The Untold Cause of Tax
Revolt</u>, by Robert Kuttner and David Kelston, 1980. Available
from the Conference on Alternative State and Local Policies,
$5.95.

<u>State Fiscal Conditions as States Entered 1982</u>, 1981,
National Conference of State Legislatures.

<u>Natural Resource Taxation: Perspectives, Resources, and
Issues</u>, 1980. Available from the Conference on Alternative State
and Local Policies, $5.95.

<u>State and Local Tax Revolt: New Directions for the '80s</u>,
edited by Dean Tipps and Lee Webb, 1981. Available from the
Conference on Alternative State and Local Policies, $9.95.

<u>Organizations</u>

ADVISORY COMMISSION ON INTERGOVERNMENTAL RELATIONS, 1111
20th St. N.W., Washington, D.C. (202) 653-5540.

CALIFORNIA TAX REFORM ASSOCIATON, 1228 1/2 H St., Sacramento,
CA, 95814 (916) 446-0145.

CITIZENS FOR TAX JUSTICE, 1825 K Street, NW, Washington, D.C.
20036 (202) 293-5430.

FEDERATION OF TAX ADMINISTRATORS, 444 N. Capitol St., Suite
334, Washington, D.C. 20002 (202) 624-5890.

MULTISTATE TAX COMMISSION, 1790 30th St., Boulder, CO, 80301
(303) 447-9645. Eugene Corrigan, Executive Director.

NATIONAL CONFERENCE OF STATE LEGISLATURES, 444 N. Capitol St.,
Suite 203, Washington,D.C., 20001 (202) 624-5000.

NATIONAL GOVERNORS ASSOCIATION, 444 N. Capitol St., Suite
250, Washington, D.C., 20001 (202) 624-5300.

Prepared by David Wilhelm.

Consumer Issues

Consumer Protection

<u>BACKGROUND FACTS</u>

The Reagan administration is dismantling consumer protections won for consumers in the recent decade.

National policy now focuses on protection of the producer, the underlying assumption being that the marketplace will protect the consumer.

The soaring cost of credit has led to a tremendous rise in costs of consumer goods. In larger states, it is estimated that every percentage increase in credit rates translates into $100 million in increased credit costs.

Homeownership is available to only about 5% of those who do not already own a home. Whereas five years ago the rule of thumb to figure individual housing costs was 25% of disposable income, that figure has doubled for millions of people.

Health care costs have outstripped already high overall inflation rates by 50%. Despite huge outlays for medical care the U.S. has the 13th highest infant mortality rate in the world.

Energy costs also permeate and increase most other consumer costs. Utility rates have more than tripled in the last five years. For millions, utility bills exceed mortgage bills. The federal government has radically reduced its investment in conservation and development of alternative energy technologies. State utility regulators have shown little creativity in encouraging energy savings and renewable energy. Profligacy remains both policy and practice.

Budget pressures at state and local levels, coupled with business opposition, have decimated public complaint handling agencies. The FTC, the FDA, the CPSC, the NHTSA, the FCC, the Department of Justice and other federal regulatory agencies for consumer protection have all suffered substantial funding losses and more cuts are likely.

<u>THE PROBLEM</u>

Consumers are "protected" by themselves and by others, in both the public and the private sectors. To the extent that individual and collective consumer self-help can be realized, the consumer is stronger. Reliance upon a self-regulating market alone cannot take care of consumer protection: public policies and programs are essential.

Consumers have not effectively focused their potential power. The current structure of our economy, skepticism of government as a legitimate and effective watchdog, and problems of public access to corporate information have slowed and complicated consumer movements. And most consumer "problems" present themselves in such ad hoc or episodic fashion that sustained interest is often difficult for many people.

The questions become, how do we empower consumers for self-"protection," and how do we "protect" consumers where the task is beyond the private state of the art?

<u>Self Protection</u>: Information is obviously essential. Intelligible market information, pratical how-to manuals, travel guides to public processes, and other such resources are indispensable tools. There is a plethora of information; the task is one of locating it, translating it and making it available. Information can assist the individual consumer in becoming aware and avoiding victimization, in recognizing and getting maximum quality in goods and services, and in becoming an effective marketplace actor, securing redress and bringing pressure for public and private reforms.

Organization for collective action also expands the power of the consumer. It permits specific consumer concerns to be tackled, and equips individuals pitted against organized market and governmental forces with the resources and organizational capacities essential to the conduct of an effective consumer campaign.

Cooperatives, one form of consumer group, well illustrate the advantages of organization. Co-ops save people money, provide a network for the dissemination of consumer information, and may become the base for other consumer interest activity.

Utility rates, energy conservation, and alternative energy development are among fundamental consumer issues that can be addressed by another form of consumer organization, a Consumers Utility Board (CUB). A CUB is a voluntary, non-profit membership organization enabled by a state legislature and funded by ratepayers through the utility billing system. These organizations, staffed by specialists, represent ratepayers' interests in rate-setting and broader energy policy proceedings.

Consumer groups are organized around auto repair, complaint mediation, health care, perinatal services, nutrition,
ownerbuilding, money-lending, campus issues, insurance abuses,
and so on. Very effective consumer action can be developed in
already existing affinity groups such as neighborhood, church,
ethnic, or senior citizen organizations. The key is identification of concerns that will attract many consumers to participate in a united endeavor.

Public Participation Protection: Consumers can exercise
significant power through membership on public advisory boards
and regulatory bodies. For example, professional and occupational licensing boards regulate millions of purveyors of consumer goods and services. A recent movement seeks to place
"public" members on such boards, even in majorities, as in
California. This sort of participation in governance can
lead to real consumer self-determination.

Public Consumer Protection: Some areas of consumer
concern require public regulation, because their scope extends
well beyond the range of actions that individuals or groups
can take to protect themselves.

Among others, this category includes food and drug
safety, auto and highway safety, money and credit practices,
and marketplace competition. But no distinct policies mandating regulation in one area and none in another exist, as
attested to by current debates. And so consumer groups are
often involved -- and needed -- at all levels.

Some state consumer protection agencies have performed
most admirably. Depending on state statute, their domain of
powers can encompass litigation, research, complaint-handling,
consumer education, legislative and administrative advocacy,
and technical assistance (for example, on co-op formation).
Such functions supplement private consumer group activity, and
develop a level of expertise and pool of financial resources
that would otherwise be very difficult to aquire. In policy-
making forums the presence of a state consumer agency --
especially if it has public and private consumer group support
-- can be wonderfully galvanizing.

Another key public consumer protection function is the
complaint-handling agency, best in operation at the local
level. When consumer complaints against businesses can be
resolved expeditiously, the economic and social climate of a
local community is both strengthened and maintained over time.

Small Claims Court is already an effective public consumer
protection agency. Further innovations, such as raising the
dollar limit, holding night and weekend sessions, and making
translators and advisors available, could solidify this
institution's reputation as a source of redress and protection.

<u>WHAT STATES CAN DO</u>

<u>Consumer Protection Agency</u>

° States should establish a strong consumer protection agency,
  with a broad range of advocacy, education, research, mediation and assistance powers. A consumer agency should be
  encouraged to develop and work closely with its consumer
  constituency to ensure both accountability and effectiveness.

<u>Consumer Representation</u>

° States should establish a Consumers Utility Board to represent consumers in agency and judicial proceedings, lobby for
  consumer interests and provide consumers with information.

° States should put a majority of "public members" on regulatory advisory bodies, especially professional licensing
  bodies and agricultural marketing boards. California has
  already done this most successfully, and other states are
  beginning to follow suit.

° States should encourage development of consumer cooperatives,
  such as California's Cooperative Development Program, or
  Wisconsin's University Center for Cooperatives.

<u>Legal Relief</u>

° States should reform the small claims court process to
  make it more a people's court. New York has enacted several
  small claims court reform laws.

° States should provide by statute for attorney's fees for
  successful litigants in consumer cases. This "private
  attorney general" approach is well-founded in legal tradition,
  and established by laws in several states.

° States should establish a network of community-based dispute
  resolution centers, to mediate minor consumer disputes and
  other neighborhood tensions. (New York City has instituted
  such mediation centers.)

<u>Other</u>

° States should initiate a thorough review of health care
  systems to address: appropriate use of technologies,
  more aggressive and less doctor-dominated health care
  personnel mixes that dominate on prevention and "wellness"
  programs, and innovative cost control measures such as
  California's new Health Cost Czar.

<u>FOR FURTHER INFORMATION</u>

<u>Publications</u>

The <u>Complete California Consumer Catalog</u>, California
Department of Consumer Affairs, $3.00. Award-winning how-to
manual on scores of standard consumer problems.

<u>A Model Act for a Residential Utility Consumer Action
Group</u>, available from The Center for Study of Responsive Law,
P.O. Box 19367, Washington, D.C. 20036.

<u>The Record on Elected and Appointed Utility Commissions,
A Public Action Report</u>, available through the Illinois Public
Action Council, 59 East Van Buren St., Chicago, IL 60605.

Consumer Federation of America Newsletter, 1314 14th St.,
Washington, D.C. 20005. The Federation also has an extensive
list of consumer publications.

<u>Organizations</u>

CALIFORNIA DEPARTMENT OF CONSUMER AFFAIRS, 1020 N St.,
Sacramento, CA, 95814, (916) 445-4465. Wide range of programs.

CENTER FOR THE STUDY OF RESPONSIVE LAW, P.O. Box 19367,
Washington, D.C. 20036. A Ralph Nader group, providing T.A.
and resources materials for consumer group issues and organizing.
Does some state and national networking.

CONSUMER EDUCATION RESOURCE NETWORK (C.E.R.N.), 1500 Wilson
Blvd., Rosslyn, VA 22209. Excellent bibliographic services.
For specific issues, CERN is the best single source of assistance.

CONSUMER FEDERATION OF AMERICA, 1314 14th St., N.W., #901,
Washington, D.C. 20005. Provides information and networking
for national, state and local consumer groups.

CONSUMERS UNION, 256 Washington St., Mt. Vernon, NY, 10550.
National membership organization, with regional offices and
education, litigation, and advocacy programs.

NATIONAL ASSOCIATION OF CONSUMER AGENCY ADMINISTRATORS, 1511
K St., N.W., Washington, D.C. 20005. Provides networking for
state and local public consumer agencies.

NATIONAL CENTER FOR THE STUDY OF PROFESSIONS, 1527 New
Hampshire Ave., N.W., Washington, D.C. 20036. Good newsletter
and materials on reforming professional and occupational
licensing processes.

Prepared by Richard Spohn.

Cooperatives

BACKGROUND FACTS

American families feel that they are worse off now than they were ten years ago. Food prices have nearly doubled. Interest rates have doubled. And energy prices have doubled.

Americans have begun to look for alternatives. Many have turned to cooperatives. One-fourth of all Americans belong to a cooperative or have a member of the immediate household who belongs. The percentage of participation ranges from 41% in the West to 16% in the East. Almost half of those who do not belong to a co-op say the reason is that there are none around that they know about.

If Americans had more co-ops available to them or knew more about them, the co-ops they would be most interested in joining, in order of preference, are food (54%), health care (27%), housing (19%), energy (18%), auto repair (18%), and child care (8%).

In 1979, nearly 3,000 cooperative food stores and buying clubs were retailing food to their member owners and others. Over 100 exist in Dallas, Texas alone.

Co-op customers save 21.7% on food costs, according to a 1981 study. Pre-order food cooperatives can deliver goods usually at a gross margin of less than 8%, whereas the average gross margin in the grocery store industry is 22%.

Health care co-op costs range up to 40% below the national average. The Group Health Cooperative of Puget Sound, for example, reports its average cost per prescription was $2.02 compared with an average in the Pacific Northwest area of $4.80.

Fuel co-ops, especially popular in the Northeast, claim savings of eight to twelve cents a gallon less than prevailing retail prices.

Housing co-ops offer home ownership opportunities to those who can least afford it. Limited equity housing co-ops offer the greatest savings; initially, they are an average of 5 to 10% less than comparable housing. Over time this savings increases to up to 50%.

Capital to start cooperatives used to be a barrier. But in 1979 Congress created the National Consumer Coopertive Bank, which operates nationwide through eight regional offices. As of June 1982, the Bank had $62.2 million in loans outstanding, and an additional $160 million in capital available for other loans.

<u>THE PROBLEM</u>

Cooperatives are businesses owned and controlled by the people who use them. They operate on a not-for-profit basis because they don't need to make a profit off themselves. Service, not profit, is their motivating force in the marketplace.

Legally, they are hybrid corporations falling in between non-profit and profit corporations. Essentially, they are non-profit corporations able to sell stock and distribute profits to their member-owners.

Although cooperatives offer consumers and their communities a tremendous opportunity, numerous obstacles exist to cooperatives' survival and expansion.

Specifically, co-ops have faced two constantly recurring problems: lack of access to adequate credit and lack of access to technical and managerial assistance. Private financing sources have been reluctant to provide this credit because the corporate structure of a cooperative is unfamiliar to them: (1) co-ops have no identifiable majority stockholder that can be held accountable and (2) co-ops are not-for-profit businesses. In addition, technical and managerial assistance that is readily available to other for profit businesses is rarely available to consumer cooperatives.

A score of serious, related problems have compounded the effects of co-ops' lack of accessible credit and technical assistance. These problems, which create a difficult environment for cooperatives, include:

° The lack of legislatively mandated state agencies that have specific statutory authority and advocacy duties for consumer cooperatives.

° The lack of public education programs that provide consumer awareness about cooperative businesses and train their future managers.

As a result, little of the normal support network so crucial to the survival and success of corporate enterprise exists for co-ops. State policies which are aimed at stimulating business, housing or health care often exclude co-ops. State regulation often either ignores co-ops' special needs or is openly hostile to their corporate structure and their needs.

     Despite the problems, cooperatives have been quite suc-
cessful in America, because they offer so many advantages.
Some of these advantages include:

° Consumer co-ops save money. They are self-help efforts.
  They distribute their earnings back to members on the basis
  of patronage, not investment. Their use of volunteers
  provides savings and skills training at the same time.

° Often cooperatives are the only way a neighborhood in the
  inner city or in rural areas can get the basic necessities.
  At one time, residents in Watts, California, had no supermar-
  ket within three square miles. Now, Watts residents own and
  control their own co-op food market.

° Cooperatives provide a training ground for members in democracy and public participation. This kind of training becomes increasingly important for average citizens to receive
  in an era of professionalism. Moreover, such training of a
  citizenry is critical to the maintenance of a pluralistic
  democracy. For example, Alabaman black farmers went on to
  field a slate of candidates for county government after they
  had successfully organized their marketing cooperative.
  Leaders of local food and housing cooperatives have frequently stepped from co-op boards to the local planning commission or city council.

° Consumer cooperatives provide constant public education.
  Co-ops in Berkeley and Chicago have pioneered in ingredient
  labeling, net weight listing, nutritional labeling, and unit
  pricing. They even staff their retail stores with full-time
  home economists to answer questions from consumers and to
  perform educational demonstrations.

     In general, the cooperative is the only method of organiza-
tion of industrial enterprise that guarantees that more regional
income stays within the region. Cooperatives also contribute
to regional self-sufficiency, and to decentralization of
wealth and of economic organization.

     Small business organizations sometimes argue that coopera-
tives have an unfair competitive edge because they do not have
to make a profit. Conservative taxpayer associations argue
that cooperatives do not pay taxes (this is because net profit
for tax purposes in cooperatives is computed after the distribution of the patronage refund). But any business which wants
to redistribute profit, or overcharge, to customers on this
basis can receive the same tax treatment.

<u>WHAT STATES CAN DO</u>

<u>General</u>

° States should establish "Task Forces on Cooperative Development" to bring together state officials and cooperative leaders to develop a state action plan for cooperative development, including suggested new legislation, elimination of harmful rules and regulations, and new program ideas for existing state agencies. Several states have set up such commissions, most notably, the Governors Task Force for Cooperative Development in Michigan.

° States should enact a separate "cooperative" section in their corporation code. Many states lack such legislation. Texas, for example, adopted a special section for the first time in 1979. California is updating its consumer cooperative code providing an excellent national model.

° States should modify their security laws to meet the unique needs of consumer cooperatives. New Mexico consumer coops achieved total exemption from securities laws in 1982.

<u>Education</u>

° States should require their state colleges and universities to create programs to train managers, staff, and boards of directors of cooperatives, similar to the programs operated by the University of Wisconsin Extension Division.

° States should establish technical assistance programs for consumer cooperatives, assisting them with accounting, management, business planning, financing, and other needed skills. The programs of California's Department of Consumer Affairs and Department of Housing and Community Development are good examples.

° State legislatures should encourage public understanding and knowledge about cooperatives by joining Congress in declaring October as "Co-op Month".

<u>Housing</u>

° States should enact general legislation limiting cooperative and condominium conversion of older buildings, to give existing tenants the first right to buy the building or individual units. Such a law should also include mobile home parks.

° States should enact legislation that would give preference in housing programs to "limited equity" housing co-ops.

° States should enact legislation making housing cooperatives eligible for mortgage financing through tax-exempt bonds.

<u>FOR FURTHER INFORMATION</u>

<u>Publications</u>

<u>Community Energy Cooperatives: How to Organize, Finance,
and Manage Them</u>, 1982, Conference on Alternative State and
Local Policies.

<u>We Own It: Starting and Managing Co-ops, Collectives,
and Employee Owned Ventures</u>, Honigsberg, Kamoroff and Beatty,
Bell Springs Publishing, Laytonville, CA 95454.

<u>An Introduction to Cooperative Conversions</u>, 1980, State
of California, Department of Housing and Community Development,
921 Tenth St., Room 102, Sacramento, CA 95814.

<u>Cooperative Housing, 1981</u>, Federal Home Loan Bank Board,
Office of Community Investment. Available from regional offices.

<u>Organizations</u>

COOPERATIVE DEVELOPMENT AND ASSISTANCE PROJECT, Conference on
Alternative State and Local Policies, 2000 Florida Ave.,
N.W., Washington, D.C. 20009 (202) 387-6030. Provides
technical assistance to low-income cooperatives.

COOPERATIVE LEAGUE OF THE USA, 1828 L St., N.W., Washington,
D.C., 20036 (202) 872-0550. Umbrella trade association for
producer and consumer cooperatives. Maintains extensive
publications list.

INDUSTRIAL COOPERATIVE ASSOCIATION, 2161 Massachusetts Ave.,
Cambridge, MA, 02140 (617) 547-4245. Helps obtain financing,
marketing and technical assistance to industrial cooperatives.

NATIONAL CONSUMER COOPERATIVE BANK, 1630 Connecticut Ave.,
Washington, D.C., 20009 (202) 745-4630. Provides loans and
technical assistance to consumer (and some producer) cooperatives through regional offices.

NATIONAL ASSOCIATION OF HOUSING COOPERATIVES, 2501 M St.,
N.W., Suite 451, Washington, D.C., 20037 (202) 887-0706.

COMMUNITY ECONOMICS, 1904 Franklin St., Oakland, CA, 94672
(415) 832-8300. National specialists in syndication and other
alternative financing sources for housing co-ops.

COOPERATIVE DEVELOPMENT PROGRAM, California State Department
of Consumer Affairs, 1020 N St., Rm. 501, Sacramento, CA
95814 (916) 322-7674. Provides publications and technical
assistance to consumer co-ops.

Prepared by Ann Evans.

Insurance

<u>BACKGROUND FACTS</u>

Insurance company assets are at the 3/4 trillion dollar level, 2.5 times the assets of the oil companies. The major insurance companies are among the largest corporations in the United States -- the chief among them, Prudential, possessing larger assets than any company save AT&T.

The industry as a whole, in 1979, employed more than 1.7 million workers.

This enormous industry, on average, represents an expenditure of over $1,000 for every man, woman and child in the country. Fully 11.4% of the nation's disposable income goes into insurance premiums.

States have nearly sole power to regulate the insurance industry. In 1945, following heavy insurer lobbying, Congress delegated regulation responsibility to the states, with no standards for state law or enforcement.

In general, states' regulatory performance has been sorely inadequate. In 1979, the General Accounting Office (GAO) found "<u>serious shortcomings</u> in state laws and regulatory activities with respect to protecting the interests of insurance consumers in the United States," noting "that insurance regulation is <u>not characterized by an arms-length relationship</u> between the regulators and the regulated." (Emphasis added.)

If insurance were truly competitive, this situation would be of less concern, but it isn't. Competition is impeded by many factors, including complexity of the product, product differentiation and lack of full disclosure of needed information. This greatly restricts competitive buying by the consumer, particularly for life insurance (where, for example, access to information concerning rates of return paid on the savings portion of their life policies is unavailable) and increases the likelihood of both poor consumer judgement and manipulation of the consumer.

In many states competition is also restricted by anti-rebate laws, which make unlawful the reduction by independent insurance agents of commission rates set by various insurance groups. The law's aim is to prevent dishonest agents from convincing the consumer to buy dubious policies by promising free gifts or rebates on the agents' commission -- commissions which, ranging from 30% to over 100%, encourage unscrupulous behavior and significantly raise consumer costs. The actual effect, however, is to stifle competition.

<u>THE PROBLEM</u>

The insurance industry is very large, very traditional, and resists change. A major lobbyist, it is very effective in Washington, and is, unarguably, the largest single lobbying force at the state level. Millions of dollars are spent each year arguing for rate increases and other changes before state insurance commissioners, and additional millions are spent lobbying state legislators and Congress. These costs are passed on to the consumers.

In many lines of insurance, cartels still either set rates for the whole market or for large shares of the market. In almost all instances they make key actuarial judgements about future economic conditions, set classes and territories, and substantially lessen the flow of competition: in all states, laws prohibit insurance agents from competing among themselves. Insurance abuses are common. The worst cases include sharp Medicare insurance salespersons who prey on the elderly, expensive industrial life insurance which is oversold to the poor, the redlining of neighborhoods, and sex discrimination which is routinely accepted.

The roots of the industry's inefficiency are manifold: Price-fixing and the absence of accountability requirements (whether to stock-holders, consumers, or, often, state regulatory agencies) are two major causes. Because antitrust statutes largely exempt the insurance industry, motivation remains towards greater growth rather than towards leaner, more streamlined operation. For many reasons, including concern for the profitability of these large employers, state regulators are anxious to keep even inefficient companies profitable. There is little motivation from any source to experiment, to innovate, to change.

While the interests of the insurance companies are well represented in the legislative and regulatory arenas, those of the consumer are not. The monolithic nature of the industry, the complexities of investigation and reform and the prohibitive costs of retaining actuaries, lawyers and other staff have effectively limited consumer action.

The Federal Trade Commission (FTC) and the Federal Insurance Administration (FIA) had, in the mid- to late-1970s, taken steps to help consumers through publication of reports on life insurance costs disclosure, redlining and other central insurance issues. Congress has moved, however, under insurance industry lobbying pressure, to deny FTC the authority even to study insurance. FIA has been restructured and has ended its pro-consumer activities.

There is some active state representation of consumer
interests. In New Jersey and South Carolina the state legislatures created a separate state agency to intervene in
insurance rate cases on behalf of consumers, and in Massachusetts, the Attorney General is a statutory intervenor on
their behalf. In these three states, intervention by experts
has demonstrably saved hundreds of millions of dollars.

In New Jersey, the function of presenting the consumer
viewpoint in rate cases, court cases and legislative matters
has, by law, been given to the Department of Public Advocate.
The costs of intervention -- such as the hiring of expert
witnesses -- is passed back to the filing insurer. The system
requires a decision by the Public Advocate on whether to intervene or not. All rate filings and other matters of interest
are required to be sent to the Public Advocate for review.
Once the Public Advocate intervenes, questions regarding the
filing, issues raised by the matter and so on are presented
to the insurance company, which must respond. Ultimately
(unless a settlement occurs), a hearing is held before the
insurance commissioners, who later renders a decision based
on input from the insurer and the Public Advocate.

In South Carolina, the process is similar. The South
Carolina Office of Consumer Advocate handles these matters.
In South Carolina, one major difference is that funding for
expert witnesses and the like is by appropriation.

In the area of public utilities, Wisconsin citizens
formed a Citizens Utility Board (CUB) which represents residential consumers on utility issus before state regulatory
agencies, the legislature and other branches of government.
The funding of the CUB is voluntary, and it receives no tax
dollars. However, an important element of CUB's enabling
legislation gives CUB the right to enclose notices in utility
bills. This gives unorganized consumers the means to organize
and protect themselves.

In insurance, a Citizens Insurnace Board (CIB) would perform similar functions and additionally, would disseminate
consumer information to help its members shop for insurance.

<u>WHAT STATES CAN DO</u>

<u>Consumer Responsiveness</u>

° States should institutionalize consumer representation in
  administrative, legislative and judicial proceedings by
  establishing Consumer Insurance Boards. The CIB would be
  funded by voluntary contributions from consumers who would
  receive notice of the organization in their bills.

° State insurance commissions should prepare consumer booklets,
  including names and rates of specific insurance companies
  and publish comparative price guides on various types of
  insurance including homeowner, automobile, life, and others.

° State insurance commissions should create a toll-free line
  for consumer complaints, should provide follow-up and back
  up to consumer complaints <u>vis a vis</u> individual insurance
  companies, and should publish surveys comparing the record
  of individual insurance companies in handling complaints.

° State insurance commissions should require that insurance
  policies be written simply and clearly, in plain, non-
  technical language.

° State insurance commissions should develop regulations,
  like those of New York State, that allow broad access to
  the election of Board of Directors' and provide for greater
  stockholder and public participation in the decisions of
  the companies.

<u>Affirmative Action</u>

° State insurance commissions should require insurance
  companies to develop affirmative action programs to promote
  women and minorities into more responsible and well-paid
  positions.

<u>Economic Development</u>

° States should enact legislation to create an insurance
  company-financed publicly chartered corporation, such as
  the Massachusetts Capital Resource Company, to provide
  loans to small businesses to create in-state jobs.

<u>Health Costs</u>

° State insurance commissions should require Blue Cross/Blue
  Shield to play a stronger role in controlling the costs of
  hospital and doctor services.

<u>FOR FURTHER INFORMATION</u>

<u>Publications</u>

Government Facilitation of Consumerism: A Proposal for Consumer Action Groups, Arthur Best and Bernard L. Brown, Temple Law Quarterly, Volume 50, 1977. (Particularly the section on Insurance and the Appendix -- An Act to Create an Insurance Consumer Action Group.)

The "Agent" and the "Arbiter": Two Important Actors on the Regulatory Stage, 1981 Harvard Business School, Cambridge, Massachusetts.

The Invisible Bankers: Everything the Insurance Industry Never Wanted You To Know, Andrew Tobias, 1982, Linden Press, $15.50.

Issues and Needed Improvements in State Regulation of the Insurance Business, U.S. Government General Accounting Office, October 9, 1979, PAD-79-72.

<u>Organizations</u>

CUB CAMPAIGN, P.O. Box 19312, Washington, D.C., 20036 (202) 387-8030. Paul A. Stern, Project Director. Works with the Wisconsin CUB, provides information to people interested in CUB's, including copies of model legislation, fact sheets, etc.

NATIONAL INSURANCE CONSUMER ORGANIZATION, 344 Commerce St., Alexandria, VA, 22314 (703) 549-8050. Robert Hunter, President. Publishes consumer guides and represents consumers in state and federal insurance matters.

NEW JERSEY DEPARTMENT OF PUBLIC ADVOCATE, 520 E. State St., P.O. Box 141, Trenton, NJ, 08625.

SOUTH CAROLINA OFFICE OF CONSUMER ADVOCATE, Department of Consumer Affairs, 2221 Devine St., P.O. Box 5757, Columbia, SC, 20250.

Prepared by Robert Hunter.

Utilities

BACKGROUND FACTS

The price of electricity is continuing to escalate even more rapidly than during the 1970s. New records were established in 1980 and 1981 when the utilities were awarded successive rate increases of $5.9 billion and $8.34 billion, more than double the previous all-time high.

In the last decade, increases in the price of electricity far outstripped the rate of inflation. Looking at national averages, a kilowatt hour selling for 1.67 cents in 1970 had nearly tripled by 1980 to 4.73 cents per kilowatt hour.

For most Americans, increases in the price of electricity have been shocking. For some, they have proved fatal. In Huntsville, Alabama, eight people including five small children died in 1982 in a fire touched off by a lighted candle after the local utility shut the family's power off when their payments fell behind. The New York Times estimated that so-called "terminations" took 200 lives in the last three years.

Utiities have been quick to blame rising fuel costs, particularly oil, as the major factor driving up electric rates. Following on the heels of the OPEC oil embargo, they were granted a record $3.1 billion in rate increases in 1975.

Due in large part to these increases, utilities' net income jumped 19.8% for 1981, and profits for the first quarter of 1982 were 21% ahead of the previous year's first quarter. For other industries across the nation, profits declined by an average of 11% during the same period.

Not content with this performance, utility industry leaders say more price increases are necessary in order for them to raise $500 billion for maintenance and construction programs through 1990.

While utility executives are trying to sell the need for more construction outlays and more generating plants, the demand for electricity has plummetted. In 1981 sales of electricity rose less than 1% (.8%), and in the first six months of 1982 sales actually declined 1.4%. Even in the unlikely event that industry projections of 4 and 5% annual growth in sales proved true, utility figures indicate that reserve generating capacity would hover around 30 per cent through the 1980's. Fifteen percent is considered an adequate reserve margin.

<u>THE PROBLEM</u>

Prior to the early 1970s electric utilities were a "de-creasing cost" industry. Because of economies of scale, electricity produced by new and larger generating plants was less costly than that produced by older plants. The utilities, therefore, agressively promoted sales by offering discount rates to large volume customers. In some cases, they offered kick-backs to contractors for building "Gold Medallion" all-electric homes. Since prices remained stable, consumers generally remained unconcerned about these expansionary practices, and the industry was doubled in size every ten years.

During the mid-1970s, however, inflation, rising fuel costs, and dramatic increases in the cost of building new generating plants made electric utilities an "increasing cost" industry. Nuclear plant construction costs were particularly staggering. Each unit of electricity produced by a new generating plant now costs more than electricity from an older plant. It has become cheaper to save a kilowatt of electricity than to generate a new one.

Nevertheless, utilities have pushed forward with construction programs, saddling not only themselves, but consumers with enormous financial burdens.

The electric utility industry has become the most capital-intensive in the economy. On an annual basis, the investor-owned utilities generally account for about 20 per cent of all new industrial construction, 33% of all corporate financing that is undertaken, and about 50% of all common stock issued. While the utilities gobble up capital, consumers meanwhile have had to respond to higher prices by cutting consumption. This situation leads to what noted energy analyst Amory Lovins describes as a "spiral of impossibility." Higher rates needed to finance new power plants drive down the demand for electricity that these plants are supposedly being built to meet.

To escape this "spiral of impossibility," utility activists have proposed reforms ranging from survival tactics -- preventing utilities from shutting off service during winter months -- to strategies that challenge the need for, and propose substitutes to, building big new central generating plants.

In the area of ratepayer rights, New York citizens won important protections when the legislature adopted a comprehensive Utility Consumers Bill of Rights in 1981. In addition to restricting winter shut-offs, this legislation also limits utilities from demanding security deposits and requires special procedures before service to senior citizens can be terminated.

Promotional rate structures intended to increase sales
by providing discount prices to large users have often been
the target of consumer wrath. More than a dozen states have
adopted a reform called "Lifeline Service," which alleviates
some of the unfairness in promotional rates by fixing a low
monthly cost for the amount of electricity needed by a typical
family.

Many utilities now petition their state utility commissions for rate increases every year. Frequently the utilities
ask permission to charge customers for plants under construction. Most state utility commissions either prohibit or nar-
rowly define this practice; Oregon, Missouri and New Hampshire
have passed legislation making it illegal.

Consumers are often at a disadvantage in challenging the
need for new power plants because only the utilities can afford
to study projected demand. Typically these forecasts overstate
demand growth. However, California and 19 other states now
require their utility commission or another state agency to
conduct formal public hearings and establish an independent
electricity forecast.

Utility reformers usually turn to the legislature when
state utility commissions prove unresponsive. In some states,
though, progressives have decided to change the way in which
commissioners are elected. Eleven states presently have elected
rather than governor-appointed commissions.

The National Energy Act of 1978, mandates utility commission review of load management techniques and automatic fuel
adjustment clauses; requires utilities to pay a fair price
for electricity they purchase from small power producers; and
requires each state to set up a Residential Conservation Service
(RCS) offering consumers free or inexpensive home energy audits.

The reforms required or suggested by the National Energy
Act, and others proposed by utility activists,could go a long
way toward saving the utilities from themselves. But utilities
have decided instead to fight the Energy Act and push ahead
with their spiraling program of more construction and more
rate increases.

Although conservation of existing energy sources and development of renewable ones hold tremendous potential, utilities continue to cling to the idea that there is an exact
correlation between expanding (and wasteful) energy use and
increases in living standards.

WHAT STATES CAN DO

To Protect Consumer Rights:

° States should establish a Bill of Rights, as in New York,
  with specific protections involving winter shutoffs, security
  deposits, and termination procedures.

° States should pass enabling legislation to create a Citizens
  Utility Board (CUB), like Wisconsin, which represents consumers
  and raises funds by placing regular notices in utility bills

° States should require utilities to pay the costs incurred by
  consumer organizations and their expert witnesses when they
  are granted intervenor status in a utility commission proceeding.

° States should require election of public utility commissioners.

To Reform Rates and Protect Against Unfair Rate Increases:

° States should eliminate promotional rate structures and replace them with "flat" rates where everyone pays the same
  price per kilowatt hour or "invested rates" where the price
  increases as use increases. In addition, states should establish a Lifeline Rate which guarantees a low, fixed monthly
  rate for necessary amounts of electricity.

° States should abolish automatic fuel adjustment charges.

° States should require utility stockholders to bear the cost of
  advertising which does not directly promote energy conservation.

° States should prohibit utilities from charging consumers for
  taxes utilities do not pay. Federal tax credits have practi-
  cally eliminated tax liability for many utilities, yet they
  are allowed to charge consumers as if they did not receive
  these tax credits.

° States should bar utilities from charging for Construction
  Work in Progress (CWIP).

To Promote Energy Efficiency and Renewable Resources:

° States should conduct annual public hearings to establish
  independent forecasts of demand for electricity.

° States should establish a Residential Conservation Service
  (RCS) program with audits performed by citizen organizations
  or other independent contractors.

° States should provide tax credits or other incentives for
  conservation and renewable energy investments.

<u>FOR FURTHER INFORMATION</u>

<u>Publications</u>

<u>Power & Light: Political Strategies for the Solar Tran-</u>
<u>sition</u>, David Talbot and Richard E. Morgan, 1981. Available
from the Environmental Action Foundation, $6.95. Tells how
citizens can work with public officials to make solar energy
and conservation happen at the local level.

<u>The Rate Watcher's Guide: How to Shape Up Your Local</u>
<u>Utility's Rate Structure</u>, Richard E. Morgan, 1980. Available
from the Environmental Action Foundation, $4.95. A handbook
for citizens seeking the reform of utility rate designs.

<u>Taking Charge: A New Look at Public Power</u>, Richard E.
Morgan, Tom Riesenberg and Michael Troutman, 1976. Available
from the Environmental Action Foundation, $4.95.

<u>The Power Line</u>, published monthly by the Environmental
Action Foundation. Regular subscription $25. Designed to keep
citizens abreast of current utility issues around the country.

<u>New Initiatives in Energy Legislation: A State by State</u>
<u>Guide, 1981-1982</u>. Available from the Conference on Alternative
State and Local Policies, $5.95.

<u>Energy Conservation and the Poor: Strategies for State</u>
<u>and Local Governments</u>, by Michael Freedberg and William Schweke,
1982. Available from the Conference on Alternative State and
Local Policies, $4.95.

<u>Model Public Utility Act</u>, by Lee Webb. Available for $2.50
from the Conference on Alternative State and Local Policies.

<u>Organizations</u>

ENVIRONMENTAL ACTION FOUNDATION, 724 Dupont Circle Building,
Washington, D.C., 20036 (202) 659-1130. The Foundation's
Energy Project publishes books, studies and information packets
designed for citizens working to reform their local utility.

CONFERENCE ON ALTERNATIVE STATE AND LOCAL POLICIES, 2000 Florida
Ave., N.W., Washington, D.C., 20009 (202) 387-6030, Lee Webb,
Director. Publishes studies on energy policy and periodic
updates on new state legislation.

AMERICAN PUBLIC POWER ASSOCIATION, 2301 M St., N.W., Washington,
D.C., 20037 (202) 775-8300. National trade organization for
municipally-owned electric utilities; publishes a monthly
magazine, <u>Public Power</u>, as well as a weekly newsletter.

Prepared by Jeff Brummer.

Human Services

Child Care

BACKGROUND FACTS

As the government reduces its support for the care of children, the demand for high quality, reasonably-priced child care is growing. By 1990, 12 million pre-schoolers will need such care.

Professional child care comes in two major forms: child care centers and child care homes. The homes are commonly know as "babysitting" or, more accurately, "family day care."

While their parents work, at least six million children in this country spend the day in some form of unregulated child care. Of the estimated 8.2 million children in child care, only 900,000 are cared for in the approximately 18,000 licensed day care centers. Some 7.3 million are kept in 2 million family day care homes, only 142,000 of which are licensed.

Despite requirements in 40 states that family day care providers be licensed, certified or registered by a state agency, less than 8% of the estimated two million family day care homes in this country are so regulated.

More than six million children receive child care in unregulated family day care homes from providers who may not be aware of basic health and safety requirements, nutrition information, or the availability of resources for children. In addition, some parents of these six million children may be ineligible for child care tax credits under the "Economic Recovery Act of 1981" because it requires that child care be provided in a licensed facility if the facility serves six children or more but says nothing about homes serving fewer than six children.

State licensing standards have often reflected noble, but unrealistic, goals. Rather than encourage family day care providers to come forward in order to gain access to information, training and technical assistance (usually available at no cost to the taxpayer), strict and forbidding licensing and zoning requirements push providers further underground.

<u>THE PROBLEM</u>

There are two basic methods used by states to regulate family day care: licensing and registration. Licensing is the granting of formal permission by a designated state or local agency to operate a child care facility. This agency has the authority to set standards, conduct inspections to insure that standards are being met, establish procedures for revoking licenses, and provide appeal mechanisms.

In addition to the inspections carried out by the licensing agency, local fire and health departments also conduct on-site inspections. Given limited state and local personnel, the licensing procedure is lengthy and sometimes expensive. Not only must state and local tax dollars be spent, but the provider herself often has to pay for the fire and/or health department inspections.

The common assumption is that licensed homes have been and continue to be monitored for various health and safety requirements such as fire inspections, cleanliness, emergency provisions, number of exits in the home, double sinks in the kitchen, number of children permitted in the home, fenced yards, separate cooking areas and planned child development activities. In reality:

° In 29 states, delays in on-site monitoring can mean that a family day care provider must wait for as long as one year to obtain her license or that her license will expire before it is renewed; and

° In 19 states, licensing requirements are so rigid and unrealistic that they act as a barrier to all but a few caregivers.

As a result, more than six million children received child care in unregulated family day care homes.

Registration is a form of regulation that stresses caregiver self-inspection and parent awareness. Where done properly, the process works as follows: registration standards, generally similar to those used in licensing, are determined by the state. When the family day care provider receives information detailing the standards, she/he does a self-study to determine whether or not the standards (including fire and health standards) are met and informs the state agency of his/her findings. Parents receive a copy of the regulations and a form for filing complaints. In many instances, inspections are not made unless the state receives a complaint.

Both licensing and registration offer some measure of the quality of child care provided and the physical condition of the homes. But such regulation of family day care has not been successful, as demonstrated by the fact that fewer than 8% of family day care homes are listed with a state agency, despite the existence of laws requiring such regulation in 40 states. The quality of care _can_ be improved, however, through a registration process aimed at raising the level of awareness of both family day care providers and parents. In addition, once a provider is listed with a state agency:

° She/he gains access to information, training and technical assistance (generally offered by nonprofit organizations, organized family day care provider associations, and universities, to providers who can be reached by mail).

° As the provider becomes better informed about proper nutrition, the availability of toy lending libraries and assistance from provider associations, the quality of the care improves.

° Parents of children in these providers' care can be sure of their eligibility for the newly increased child care tax credit under the "Economic Recovery Tax Act of 1981."

Whatever the preference -- family day care homes or child care centers -- it is essential to protect the health and well being of children in care as well as to protect the rights of the child caregiver. In an economy that increasingly requires parents to work, it is incumbent upon state and local officials to propose and support measures that make as many forms of quality child care available as possible.

WHAT STATES CAN DO

Children and Youth Agency

° States should establish an agency for children and youth.
  In some states, like Massachusetts, this kind of agency
  is already established in the Governor's office. The
  agency should also provide services that support family
  day care homes such as: training and technical assistance
  to providers; referral services for providers and parents;
  a list of family day care providers to corporations and
  businesses for use by their employees; encouragement of
  day care centers to support and assist family day care
  homes; and inclusion of providers in conferences and boards
  of this agency.

Licensing and Registration

° States should alter their licensing and registration processes to allow for a more flexible registration process
  to encourage unregulated family day care providers to
  become regulated. All family day care homes should be
  required to register. Family day care homes should be
  monitored on a random sample and on the basis of complaints
  received. Georgia state recognized this problem and, after
  several years with a virtually unenforceable licensing
  law, switched to registration in 1980.

  In Texas, when licensing was in effect, only 15 to 20
  homes a month were licensed. Now, with registration, an
  average of 200 homes are registering with the state each
  month. Since registration was instituted in Massachusetts
  in 1974, the number of regulated homes has increased from
  862 to 5,100.

° States should encourage and assist non-profit organizations, universities, etc., that attempt to provide services
  to family day care providers.

° States should establish outreach services aimed at encouraging providers to register. This should be done in cooperation
  with community groups, non-profit organizations concerned
  with child care and associations of family day care providers.

Zoning

° States should pass legislation creating a zoning variance
  that permits family day care homes to operate regardless
  of existing zoning regulations. Minnesota has passed such
  a law. Unless this is done, many providers will continue
  to operate outside of the law.

<u>FOR FURTHER INFORMATION</u>

<u>Publications</u>

     <u>Handbook of Family Day Care Associations</u>, January, 1981, The Children's Foundation, 1420 New York Ave., N.W., Suite 800, Washington, D.C., 20005, $1.00. Annotated directory of state and local family day care associations.

     <u>Family Day Care Licensing Study</u>, The Children's Foundation, 1420 New York Ave., N.W., Suite 800, Washington, D.C., 20005, (forthcoming), $3.00. State-by-state analysis of licensing and regulation of family day care in the continental U.S.

<u>Organizations</u>

THE CHILDREN'S FOUNDATION, 1420 New York Ave., N.W., Suite 800, Washington, D.C., 20005 (202) 347-3300. Barbara Bode, President. A national organization working to ensure economic opportunity and access to decision-making processes for American families, particularly low- and moderate-income women and their children.

NATIONAL BLACK CHILD DEVELOPMENT INSTITUTE, 1463 Rhode Island Ave., N.W., Washington, D.C., 20005 (202) 387-1281. Evelyn K. Moore, Executive Director. A national nonprofit membership organization that couples public policy advocacy with an affiliate network to promote programs to assist the develoment and welfare of Black children.

CHILDREN'S DEFENSE FUND, 1520 New Hampshire Ave., N.W., Washington, D.C., 20036 (202) 483-1470. Marian Wright Edelman, President. A national child advocacy organization that seeks reforms in the treatment, care and education of children; also involved in lobbying and litigation.

NATIONAL ASSOCIATION FOR FAMILY DAY CARE, 41 Dunbar St., Manchester, NH, 02103 (503) 622-4408. Jeffrey Kent, Interim Coordinator. A newly formed provider run association promoting the quality of family day care so that the best possible services are offered to children, parents and providers.

CHILD CARE RESOURCE CENTER, 187 Hampshire St., Cambridge, MA, 02139 (617) 547-9861. Works to expand the availability of parent and worker controlled child care, providing referrals and other support services.

Prepared by Barbara Bode.

The Elderly

<u>BACKGROUND FACTS</u>

Nearly 26 million people in the United States are 65 or older--more than 11% of our total population. From 1970 to 1979, the number of older Americans increased almost four times as rapidly as the under-65 age group (23.5% vs. 6.3%).

Each day, there is a net increase of 1600 Americans 65 or older. This translates to about a 600,000 annual increase in the 65-plus population.

The number of older Americans is expected to increase markedly in the years ahead, particularly during the first third of the 21st century. Almost 32 million Americans will be 65 or older by the year 2000. And by the year 2030--less than 50 years away--more than 55 million persons in the U.S. will be 65 or older, and that would constitute 18% of our total population.

6.3 million Americans 65 or older (poverty and near poverty figures do not add because of rounding) were either poor or marginally poor in 1980. That figure represents nearly 26% of all older Americans.

Older Americans are subject to more disability, see physicians 50% more often, and have twice as many hospital stays that last almost twice as long as those of younger persons.

In 1978, health care costs for the elderly totaled $49.4 billion. On a per capita basis, this amounts to $2,026 for every person 65 or older, or 3.4 times the $597 per capita average for an under-65 individual.

Many older Americans now find themselves in virtually impossible housing situations. Rising enery costs, property taxes, and maintenance expenses are making it difficult for them to remain in their homes.

Older women constitute 59% of all Americans 65 or older, but nearly 72% of all the aged persons living in poverty. About 19% of all women 65 or older were poor in 1980, compared to 11% for older men.

<u>THE PROBLEM</u>

To be an older person in America today is to be subject to a growing array of frustrations and problems. Along with the problems every American faces the elderly confront the critical problem of maintaining their standard of living, with limited resources, fixed incomes, and fragile health.

A few examples illustrate the range of difficulties older people face each day:

° Condominium conversion of rental properties occupied by senior citizens requires them to find inexpensive, convenient, safe residences in a tight housing market.

° Cutbacks in transportation services and subsidies strand persons who cannot or will not drive. Transportation is an even more serious problem in rural areas with little public transportation.

° Rising costs in energy, food, housing and health care, coupled with reductions in programs designed specifically for the elderly in these areas, force them to make impossible choices among necessities.

° Age discrimination and high levels of unemployment limit income potential.

Of all the problems encountered by the elderly, obtaining adequate and reasonably-priced health care is one of the most pressing. Health care costs are growing at twice the rate of the rest of the economy, with the elderly accounting for an increasing share of the bill.

The elderly's acute health care (short-term) needs are largely satisfied by Medicare. However, because their problems are often chronic, many older people also need long-term care services not generally required by the younger population. Consequently, the need for -- and current lack of -- long-term care services is an especially critical problem.

Long-term care includes a range of medical and supportive services for individuals who have lost some capacity for self-care due to a chronic illness or condition and will probably need extended care. At present, long-term care is typically associated with nursing homes. Nursing homes, however, are often not "homes" but sterile, impersonal institutions providing substandard care. And while only five percent of

the elderly population reside in nursing homes, up to 50% of
these people could receive care more appropriate to their
conditions outside a nursing home.

Despite the public perception of nursing homes as the
major provider of long-term care, the vast preponderance of
care for the elderly is provided by family and friends. To
aid these caregivers, and for the elderly person living
alone, there should exist a wide range of community-based
services designed specifically for the elderly. Such services
should include adult day care, in-home care, homemaker/chore
services, personal care, counseling, and nutritional programs.
To a very limited extent, these services are available through
such programs as the Community Services Block grant (formerly
Title XX) and the Older Americans Act.

Unfortunately, because resources are so limited, in many
states alternative services that would allow the elderly to
remain at home do not exist or are rare. This often requires
premature and inappropriate admission to a nursing home. Once
in the nursing home, the older person can suffer not only
from chronic illness, but also from questionable care and
treatment.

In response, state governments have enacted a wide range
of long-term care programs. To address the problems found in
their nursing homes, Illinois, Minnesota and Michigan have
enacted nursing home reform legislation that regulates and
attempts to improve the quality of care. A number of other
states, such as Connecticut, Washington, and Florida have
provided funding to establish community-based service systems
for the elderly.

Critics claim that providing a coordinated system of
care will increase public costs. Inevitably, they say, many
elderly persons who now need these services but do not have
access to them would use them. However, the availability of
these services could preclude the necessity of more costly
nursing home admissions in a significant number of cases,
thus saving money in the long run.

<u>WHAT STATES CAN DO</u>

<u>Provide Long-Term Care In the Least Restrictive Setting:</u>

° States should adopt a Medicaid provision that covers a
  wide range of home- and community-based services as an
  alternative to nursing home care. This would help reduce
  the institutional bias associated with Medicaid.

° States should provide funds to develop or maintain service
  programs to prevent premature, inappropriate institutionalization of the elderly. These could be home-delivered
  services, multi-service senior center programs, family
  placement service programs and/or day care programs.

° States should allow family allowances, personal care reimbursement, tax deductions and/or tax credits for families
  that provide major support to an elderly person. This
  would be incentive for families to continue to care for
  elderly relatives at home.

° States should create a State Joint Committee on Long-Term
  Care Alternatives to study their costs and effectiveness.

<u>Protect Rights of Residents and Ensure Quality of Care in
Institutions:</u>

° States should enact comprehensive laws regulating nursing
  homes. Provisions should, for example, include access to
  facilities by visitors, a residents bill of rights, nursing
  aid training requirements and enforcements measures.

° States should establish a nursing home ombudsman program
  to oversee nursing home activities and investigate complaints.

<u>Ensure Availability of Appropriately Trained Health Care
Providers:</u>

° States should require physicians, osteopaths, and chiro-
  practors to indicate whether they will accept Medicare
  reimbursement as payment for services to Medicare eligibles.

° States should enact upgraded geriatric licensing laws for
  physicians, nurses and other professionals who treat the
  elderly.

<u>Protect the Elderly From Questionable Insurance Sales Tactics:</u>

° States should enact laws strictly regulating the sale of
  health insurance policies sold to supplement Medicare.
  This would protect the elderly from the cost of duplicative
  policies and unnecessary coverage.

Publications

Alternatives to Institutional Care for the Elderly: An Analysis of State Initiatives, Gail Toff. Published by the Intergovernmental Health Policy Project of George Washington University. Describes successful state programs.

Legislative Approaches to Problems of the Elderly: A Handbook of Model State Statutes, Legislative Research Center of the University of Michigan Law School, Ann Arbor, MI, William J. Pierce, Director. March 1971.

Living in a Nursing Home: A Complete Guide for Residents, Their Families and Friends, Sarah Greene Burger and Martha D'erasmo.

Long-Term Care, Background and Future Directions, U.S. Department of Health and Human Services, Health Care Financing Administration, 1981. General information about long-term care.

Organizations

AMERICAN ASSOCIATION OF RETIRED PERSONS, 1909 K St., N.W., Washington, D.C., 20049, (202) 872-4200. Has a state legislation department active in elderly issues across the country.

BUREAU OF AGING, Department of Social and Health Services, OB-43G, Olympia, WA, 98504, (206) 753-2502. Administers Senior Citizens Services Act, enacted in 1976.

CENTER FOR COMMUNITY CHANGE, Block Grant Coalition, 1000 Wisconsin Ave., N.W., Washington, D.C. 20007, (202) 332-0822. Monitors state activity involving implementation of block grants.

NATIONAL CITIZENS COALITION FOR NURSING HOME REFORM, 1424 16th St., N.W., Washington, D.C., 20036, (202) 797-8227. Expertise on nursing home issues, including state legislative activities.

NATIONAL COUNCIL OF SENIOR CITIZENS, 925 15th St., N.W., Washington, D.C., 20005, (202) 347-8800. Advocates on behalf of the elderly, with expertise in health and housing issues.

OFFICE OF AGING AND ADULT SERVICES, Department of Health and Rehabilitataive Services, 1321 Winewood Blvd., Tallahassee, FL, 32301, (904) 488-8341. Responsible for implementing recently enacted Community Care for the Elderly Act.

Prepared by Joanna Chusid

Health Care

Despite a continuing decline in death rates, differences in health care between rich and poor remain. Child deaths, death from chronic diseases (stroke, peptic ulcers, bronchitis, respiratory cancers, and cancers of the stomach and esophagus) and deaths from accidents are all more common among the economically deprived.

° The infant mortality rate continued to decline, reaching 13.8 deaths per 1,000 live births in 1978. The mortality rate for black infants, however, is still almost twice as high as for white infants.

° Age-adjusted mortality rates continue to decline. However, in 1978, they remained 80% higher for men than for women and 48% higher for blacks than for whites.

° Use of doctors offices and hospital clinics is considerably lower in nonmetropolitan areas. Furthermore, residents of counties that did not have a city with a population of 10,000 or more generally had lower usage rates than other nonmetropolitan areas.

° Although there has been a marked trend toward equality in the use of physician services by income group, people in lower income groups use considerably fewer dental services than those in higher income groups.

° In 1980, health care expenditures in the United States totaled $247.2 billion -- an average of $1,067 per person, and 9.5% of the Gross National Product.

° In March, 1982, when the Consumer Price Index actually declined for the first time in years, the index for medical care continued to be over 12% per year.

° The major portion of government health care expenditures are for institutional care. For Medicare, hospital care accounted for 74% of expenditures in 1980.

° Medicaid pays for medical care for 25 million elderly persons, 5 million disabled persons, 9 million poor children, and 4 million unmarried, low-income parents.

     Public health programs targeted at special health problems
of special populations have contributed to the improved health
of Americans and have reduced the discrepancies between rich
and poor, white and non-white, and urban and rural Americans.
These programs suffer as hospital care and nursing home care
consume most of the health budgets.

     Less than two percent of health expenditures go for public
health programs such as childhood immunizations, venereal
disease and tuberculosis control, fluoridation, family planning, community mental health centers, and alcohol and drug
abuse treatment. Yet these programs are far more cost-effective than hospital care.

     States have always been responsible for public health.
The federal government has contributed funds, but state
governments have had the basic statutory responsibility for
health. The federal medical care programs -- Medicare and
Medicaid -- have grown far more rapidly than public health,
confronting Congress and state legislators with a health
system that is dominated by treatment and cure rather than
by prevention.

     One major consequence of the medical thinking has been
the denigration of active prevention efforts. Instead of
looking for health problems that can be prevented by social
action (such as cleaning up water supplies and removing
hazardous wastes), there is a new focus on individual life-
styles. This "blame the victim" approach makes it the responsibility of the worker to protect himself from hazards in the
workplace; the responsibility of the individual to quit
smoking, to eat correctly, and to exercise; and, when disease
strikes the responsibility of the victim for having failed
to prevent it. State leaders must reinstate the proper
policy role for effective public health programs if we are
to preserve the health of our people.

     Medical care costs: The growing public demand for medical
services has been fostered and responded to by a growing
medical establishment. Health is the second largest sector
of the economy; in many towns or cities hospitals are the
largest employers. This has made it almost as difficult to
redirect the medical establishment as to trim the military-
industrial complex.

     Hospital care expenditues continue to claim the largest
share of the health care dollar, accounting for 40% of total
health care expenditures in 1980. Physician services and
nursing home care accounted for 19% and 8.4%, respectively.

Because medical care is so expensive, the right to
medical care is critical for almost everyone. Great progress
has been made in assuring access to medical care. Massive
income transfers take place through private health insurance
and government health insurance (Medicare and Medicaid).
The "national health tax" -- the combination of tax money
spent on government health programs and health insurance
premiums paid by corporations and individuals -- is the
second largest "tax" system after the personal income tax.
Yet, unlike actual tax money, these funds are spent without
deliberation, without planning, and without accountability.

The problem best addressed at the state level is protecting the right to medical care -- but without unintended
growth of non-productive parts of the health establishment.
Hospital costs are still rising at the rate of 18% per year.

<u>Enforcement of the public commitment to health:</u> There
is strong evidence from opinion polling that the American
people are deeply committed to protecting the public health.
They oppose weakening of environmental and public health
statutes Yet state leaders have been slow to recognize the
opportunity to strengthen laws and programs For example, at a
recent meeting of state health officers, the prevailing fear
about toxic wastes was labeled "public hysteria." Repeatedly
these public health officials admitted to themselves the real
danger, but were unwilling to undertake a program to manage
the hazard because of the fear that they could not deal with
the public response.

Nursing homes have been a national scandal for almost
two decades, yet the Reagan administration has proposed
deregulating the industry It is an industry where the profit
comes from the real estate transactions,and where patients --
the most vulnerable people in our society -- are often abused
or neglected. The public would like stronger protections.
Because the abuses are still so clear, there is room for
aggressive reform.

<u>WHAT STATES CAN DO</u>

<u>Public Health</u>

° States should give public health and prevention the highest
  priority in their planning and budgeting. To do this states
  must analyze and duplicate the programs that work such as
  immunizations, fluoridation, feeding programs (WIC), and
  crippled childrens' programs; maintenance programs for the
  elderly; and programs for protection from environmental
  hazards.

<u>Health Costs</u>

° States should act to increase the accountability of Blue
  Cross/ Blue Shield (dominated by physicians and other
  health industry professionals) to the public as a means of
  controlling rapidly rising health insurance costs. Michigan
  law requires that three-quarters of "the Blues'" state
  board of directors be subscribers.

° States should institute "rate setting" programs to review
  hospital budgets and control the rates of growth of expenditures. Such initiatives have been successful in Maryland,
  Massachusetts, and New Jersey. These programs are most
  effective when linked to certificate of need programs that
  allocate new capital expenditures for the provision of needed
  services.

° States should encourage health maintenance organizations
  (HMOs) which discourage the use of expensive hospital services, while providing more benefits in ambulatory care
  than normal insurances.

<u>Enforcement</u>

° States should strengthen enforcement programs to protect
  public health. Tough law enforcement programs to attack
  problems such as toxic waste dumps, substandard nursing
  homes, radiation hazards and air pollution could produce
  improvements in public health.

<u>Home Health</u>

° States should adopt home health plans for the elderly and
  mentally retarded under waivers from Medicaid institutional
  care requirements. Kansas, Montana, Oregon and Louisiana
  have received waivers to reimburse the cost of home health
  care as an economical alternative to institutional care.

<u>FOR FURTHER INFORMATION</u>

<u>Publications</u>

     "Who Needs Medicaid?" David E. Rogers, Robert J. Blendon
and Thomas W. Moloney, <u>New England Journal of Medicine</u>, Vol.
307, July 1, 1982.

     <u>A New Perspective on the Health of Canadians</u>, Marc Lalonde,
National Health and Welfare, Ottawa, Canada, 1974. Good
overview of preventable health problems.

     <u>Policy Memo on a State Health Plan</u>, available fall, 1982
from the Conference on Alternative State and Local Policies,
2000 Florida Avenue, N.W., Washington, D.C. 20009. Describes
a comprehensive state health insurance plan to cover all Oregon
residents.

<u>Organizations</u>

CHILDRENS DEFENSE FUND, 1520 New Hampshire Ave., N.W.,
Washington, D.C., 20036 (202) 483-1470.

AMERICAN PUBLIC HEALTH ASSOCIATION, 1015 15th St., N.W.,
Washington, D.C., 210005 (202) 789-5600. APHA also has about
50 state affiliates.

CENTER FOR POLICY RESEARCH, National Governor's Association,
444 N. Capitol Street, Washington, D.C., 20001 (202) 624-5354.
The Center has a State Medicaid Information Center and sponsors
research on state health policy.

INTERGOVERNMENTAL HEALTH POLICY PROJECT, George Washington
University, Washington, D.C. 20006. Publishes <u>State Health
Notes</u> monthly and other reports occasionally.

PUBLIC CITIZEN HEALTH RESEARCH GROUP, 2000 P St., N.W.,
Seventh Floor, Washington, D.C., 20036, (202) 872-0320.
Publishes numerous studies on health care policy, drugs and
medical technology.

NATIONAL ASSOCIATION OF COMMUNITY HEALTH CENTERS, INC., 1625
Eye Street, N.W., Suite 420, Washington, D.C. 20006 (202) 833-
4280. Clearinghouse for information on community health center
legislation and budgets.

Prepared by Anthony Robbins.

Housing

<u>BACKGROUND FACTS</u>

The U.S. is currently facing a major crisis in housing. Annual housing starts are at their lowest rate since the late 1960's. The construction of rental housing does not meet demand. Consumers are forced to pay increasing portions of their income toward housing. Interest rates are at historic highs, and savings and loan associations -- the traditional source of financing for housing -- are in trouble.

Housing starts in the U.S. are down because interest rates are high. Housing starts in 1982 will be about 950,000 units nationwide -- almost 35 percent less than the 1.3 million starts in 1980. The rental unit construction has dwindled since the early 1970's because costs of construction surpass renters' ability to pay. Federal cut-backs in subsidized rental housing programs will further diminish the rental construction rate.

The effective mortgage interest rate for conventional new homes was almost 16 percent. High interest rates are preventing developers from building marketable housing and stopping consumers from buying new or existing housing. High interest rates have caused a 25 percent decline in rehabilitation nationwide.

Demolitions and condominium conversions are shrinking the number of rental units while rental costs continue to climb. Rent to income ratios are steadily rising. In 1950, 32 percent of all renters paid more than 25 percent of their income for rent; in 1979, more than half did. Affordability is an especially serious problem for low- and moderate-income families.

Savings and loans are in trouble. Rising inflation has confronted many lenders with serious cash flow problems. Interest rates due on deposits have risen to unexpectedly high levels while the interest received on mortgages and other assets has lagged behind. Thrift institutions are experiencing a net outflow of funds as savers rush to other more lucrative investments, such as money market funds.

The Reagan administration is cutting back on every federal housing program. A third of the total fiscal year 1982 budget cuts come from federally-assisted housing programs. The Administration is also slashing financing for construction and rehabilitation of sewers, streets, and water systems.

<u>THE PROBLEM</u>

The current housing crisis is caused by an array of problems:

<u>Affordability</u>: Prices are so high that first-time home-buyers cannot accumulate down payments or make monthly payments on current interest rates. Renters are paying increasing portions of their incomes for rent -- leaving less money for food and medical care.

<u>Availability</u>: Construction of all types of housing is down, particularly in fast growing areas such as the Sunbelt. There is tremendous pent-up demand.

<u>Financing</u>: Interest rates are preventing construction and purchases. Savings and loans may no longer be a steady source of capital. The long-term, fixed rate mortgage is disappearing. Assumable loans have essentially been banned. "Creative financing" -- potentially very dangerous for both sellers and buyers -- is proliferating.

<u>Quality</u>: Housing in some parts of the country, particularly the northeast, needs to be rehabilitated.

<u>Displacement</u>: Demand for housing in areas close to central cities has increased. Many lower-income people are being displaced from their neighborhoods through rent increases and/or evictions, and through condominium conversions.

<u>Speculation</u>: Demand for housing as both an investment and as shelter has driven prices up. Speculation has played a part in the high price of land, houses, and apartment buildings.

<u>Tenant protections</u>: As homeownership becomes more difficult, longer-term tenancy is becoming more prevalent for families.

State officials must develop responses to housing problems, as well as working to keep the federal government involved in housing financing. They should advocate continued use of mortgage revenue bonds and lobby against banning the use of federal funds in communities with housing policies such as rent control and condominium conversion ordinances.

State responses to housing problems may take a variety of forms such as: permitting innovative local land use and regulatory techniques at the local level; preventing exclusionary zoning; promoting expedited permit processes; making land and infrastructure available for housing; promoting the use of manufactured housing; promoting building codes that protect health and welfare but do not add excessive costs; financing construction and rehabilitation of housing; strengthening landlord-tenant law to increase tenant protection; and promoting cooperative ownership arrangements.

States should take an active role in financing programs to maximize the use of federal funds and sponsor programs more carefully tuned to local needs. Another reason for states to continue or start housing programs is that with federal cutbacks, the state programs may be the "only game in town."

In these times of fiscal austerity, regulatory approaches and programs to make maximum use of existing housing should be endorsed. Saving the affordable housing a community has is cheaper than subsidizing new construction of low- and moderate-income units. In light of the lack of funds, local ordinances that control rents, condominium conversions, speculation, and inclusionary zoning and that permit splitting up single family homes for "second units" should not be prevented by state action. State legislation permitting innovative local land use and regulatory techniques should be passed.

There are two traditional arguments against federal and state housing programs: that they cost too much and that the private market can take care of the problems of low- and moderate-income people.

Proponents of federal and state housing financing argue that the free market does not take care of all housing problems -- and therefore, some government action is necessary. Nor are housing programs terribly expensive; the funds spent on low- and moderate-income housing programs are nowhere near the funds lost to the U.S. Treasury through mortgage interest deductions.

Opponents of the regulatory approach to conserving low- and moderate-income housing at the local level charge that these local initiatives thwart the "free market" and keep it from providing housing for all income groups. Proponents of regulatory programs such as rent control, condominium conversion, demolition ordinances and inclusionary zoning reply that the private market often does not meet the needs of low- and moderate-income people. Thus, such policies are needed to conserve affordable housing.

<u>WHAT STATES CAN DO</u>

<u>Encouraging Affordable Housing at the Local Level</u>

° States should pass legislation permitting innovative local
  techniques such as mixed use development, density bonuses,
  inclusionary zoning, and the division of single family homes
  for second units. California has passed legislation requiring localities to grant a 25% increase in permitted density
  in project where 25% of the units will be affordable for
  low-and moderate-income people.

° States should prevent exclusionary zoning techniques.

° States should promote or not prohibit local policies to
  conserve affordable housing, such as rent control and condominium conversion ordinances.

° States should promote expedited permit processes. Virginia
  mandates a maximum of 120 days for granting of all subdivi-
  sion permits. California permits local governments to consol-
  idate all permits into one administrative process.

<u>Financing Housing</u>

° States should help finance housing. California operates numerous housing finance programs, funded through
  the general fund and through the sale of tax exempt
  mortgage revenue bonds. Connecticut, Minnesota and Wisconsin
  operate active rehabilitation funds. New Jersey operates a
  neighborhood improvement program.

  Connecticut, North Carolina and California are exploring
  the use of public pension funds for purchase of mortgage-
  backed, pass-through securities. California and Hawaii
  permit use of public pension funds for members' mortgages.
° States should make land and infrastucture available for
  housing. Connecticut, Florida, and California all provide
  low-interest loans for the purchase and development of land
  for low- and moderate-income housing.

<u>Protecting Tenants</u>

° States should strengthen tenant protections. New Jersey
  has strong just-cause eviction protections. Twelve states
  require interest to be paid to tenants on security deposits.

° States should promote cooperative ownership. New York and
  California have encouraged the financing and development of
  such cooperatives, for low- and middle-income people.

<u>FOR FURTHER INFORMATION</u>

<u>Publications</u>

State Actions for Affordable Housing, prepared for HUD Office of the Assistant Secretary for Policy Development and Research, Washington, D.C.

Housing Affairs Letter, newsletter published by Community Development Publications, 8555 16th St., Silver Spring, MD 20910.

The Housing Crisis: A Strategy for Public Pension Funds, Robert Schur and Marilyn Phelan, 1982. Available for $5.95 from the Conference on Alternative State and Local Policies.

Packaging Mortgage Loans: Strategies for California, John C. Harrington, 1980. Available for $5.95, from the Conference on Alternative State and Local Policies.

Moderate Rent Control: The Experience of U.S. Cities, John Gilderbloom, 1980. Available for $4.95, from the Conference on Alternative State and Local Policies.

Rent Control: A Source Book, John Gilderbloom and Friends, 1981. Available for $9.95 from the Conference on Alternative State and Local Policies.

Shelterforce, available to individuals at $8 for 6 issues, $12 to libraries, law offices, and institutions, 380 Main St., East Orange, NJ, 07018.

<u>Organizations</u>

HOUSING ASSISTANCE COUNCIL, INC., 1025 Vermont Ave., N.W., Suite 606, Washington, D.C. 20005, (202) 842-8600. Active in rural housing issues.

NATIONAL HOUSING LAW PROJECT, 2150 Shattuck Ave., Suite 300, Berkeley, CA, 94704, (405) 548-9400.

NATIONAL LOW-INCOME HOUSING COALITION, 215 Eighth St., N.E., Washington, D.C., 20002, (202) 544-2544.

NATIONAL TENANTS UNION/SHELTERFORCE, 380 Main St., East Orange, NJ, 07018, (201) 678-6778. Membership organization of housing activists and public officials.

PLANNERS NETWORK (Housing and Neighborhoods Task Force), P.O. Box 4671, Sather Gate Station, Berkeley, CA, 94704.

Prepared by Marilee Hanson and Lenny Goldberg.

Natural Resources and Environment

Agriculture

<u>BACKGROUND FACTS</u>

The American food system is today in an increasingly vulnerable position. Several trends are threatening to both farmers and consumers:

° Farmers presently face the worst economic situation since the Great Depression. Total farm income was $32.7 billion in 1979, fell sharply to $19.9 billion in 1980 and $22.9 billion in 1981, and in 1982 could be as low as $15 billion.

° About 3 million acres of the 540-million acre cropland are lost each year to suburban development, lakes, highways, shopping centers and other non-farm uses.

° Consumer food prices seem to be on a constantly rising course, while farm income is currently at near-depression levels. On average the farmer gets less than 40 cents of the consumer's food dollar.

° Farm debt and loan delinquencies are rising. At the beginning of 1982 over half of Farmers Home Administration one-year farm operating loans were delinquent.

° Economic clout is becoming concentrated among fewer farms. About one-fifth of all farms now account for four-fifths of total farm sales.

° The average farm size has been increasing for decades. In 1940 it was 175 acres; today it is over 400.

° Farmers are losing control over production and marketing of their crops and livestock. They must buy inputs from and sell their products to dominant large corporations.

° Farmers are growing older; their average age is now over 50.

<u>THE PROBLEM</u>

Agriculture in the United States was once a relatively simple pursuit, as it remains in the "underdeveloped" Third World. In the past farmers using relatively simple technologies produced food and fiber that was, for the most part, consumed locally or regionally. Today that system is radically different. A much smaller number of farmers raise more food on larger farms. Production is intensive, highly mechanized, dependent on large capital outlays, very specialized by region and on individual farms, and heavily reliant on chemical fertilizers, pesticides, herbicides and energy. Ownership and operation of farms are diverging, as outside investors enter the sector and as the cost of owning a farm rises above the means of most.

Food marketing today is also very different from the distribution system of a few decades ago. Consumers now buy tomatoes shipped thousands of miles as production concentrates in some areas. In addition, many farmers now export large parts of their crop.

All of this change has resulted in a food system of prodigious efficiency and productivity. We have strawberries in January, but at what cost? Beneath the successes -- and often rising above them -- are numerous flaws: unstable farm income, consumer dissatisfaction, disappearing family farms, soil erosion, farmland loss, and water depletion.

The food distribution system has become fully industrialized. Now the system of production -- farming itself -- is also on the verge of industrialization. This may or may not lead to greater efficiency. But replacement of family farms by larger production units with hired workers, farm managers and absentee owners will also aggravate major problems or create new ones. For example, research shows that when family farms decline rural communities and small businesses also suffer.

For more than a hundred years government has undertaken programs and policies aimed at supporting or rescuing agriculture generally and the family farm specifically. A vast array of federal programs has helped agriculture since the 1860s. Price supports, tax breaks, research, extension education, subsidized credit and marketing aids are only the most prominent efforts.

Yet in many ways the laws and regulations have fueled some of the most unfortunate trends in contemporary agriculture.

For example, many of the programs have helped mainly the
larger farmers, or have even enticed non-farm investors and
corporations into agriculture as competitors against the family
farm. Further complicating this picture is the Reagan administration's budget cuts in domestic programs. The few agricultural programs of real benefit to small farm operators or consumers are being cut back or face the threat of cuts. State
governments have a responsibility to fill at least some of the
breach.

    Some states have adopted one of more pieces of a progres-
sive agenda for agriculture, and many excellent ideas are
under consideration.

° For example, to keep cropland in farming Oregon requires
  that local governments have exclusive farm use zoning plans.

° In West Virginia there is a state-run system of farmers'
  markets in major cities.

° Eight states restrict non-family farm corporate ownership
  of farmland.

° Missouri and Texas have small farm extension programs which
  specifically reach out to help limited-resource operators.

    Many of those who approve of current trends in agriculture
believe that bigger is better, that growth in farm size is
necessary and inevitable, that in the past there were too many
people in farming, and that chemicals are essential to high
productivity. It is true that many very small farms cannot
achieve economic viability through agriculture alone. But
farms do not have to be enormous to achieve maximum economies
of size. For example, research by the U.S. Department of
Agriculture shows that in 1979 full efficiency was achieved on
a grain farm with annual sales of $133,000 and size of 314
acres. Growth beyond that size adds to sales and profits,
but not to increased efficiency.

    Chemicals have greatly increased yields over the last
several decades. But they have also become very expensive,
caused environmental deterioration, depleted the soil, led to
poison-resistant pests and created other problems. A mixed
use of chemical -- that is, "conventional" -- and organic products would be a much better practice.

<u>WHAT STATES CAN DO</u>

<u>Preservation of Agricultural Land</u>

° States should adopt comprehensive, integrated plans to keep
  productive land in farming. Plans could include exclusive
  agricultural zoning, tax incentives for farmland retention,
  and public purchase of the rights to land development for
  non-farm purposes.

<u>Economic and Credit Assistance</u>

° States should examine ways of rescuing the economically
  beleaguered farmer. State farm lending programs could
  supplement federal aid. Some taxes on agriculture might be
  forgiven. And land banks could be formed to buy land from
  those who must sell. A bank could resell only to family
  farmers or hold the land out of production to improve prices.

° States should establish programs to provide credit at reasonable terms to low-equity and beginning farmers. Ten states
  now have such programs. Included in such an effort should
  be (1) a partial interest subsidy; and (2) requirements that
  borrowers have both farming skills and a net worth below
  some reasonable ceiling.

<u>Marketing</u>

° States should begin or improve direct marketing programs.
  Existing markets, parking lots, shopping centers and other
  facilities could serve as market sites, where local farmers
  bring their produce for direct sale to consumers.

° States should require hospitals, schools and other public
  institutions to buy or attempt to buy locally-grown food.

<u>Research and Extension</u>

° States should attempt to refocus their research and extension systems more toward the needs on small and moderate-
  sized farms. Each state extension service should have a
  small farm program with paraprofessional aids.

° States also should ensure that their research and extension
  activities include investigation of organic agriculture and
  other small-scale, energy-efficient alternatives.

<u>The Structure of Farming</u>

° States should place limits on non-family farm corporate and
  absentee ownership of agricultural assets. Family farm corporations should be exempt from any such limits. Foreign
  ownership of farmland should be monitored and, if necessary,
  controlled.

<u>FOR FURTHER INFORMATION</u>

<u>Publications</u>

Assisting Beginning Farmers: New Programs and Responses, 1980, Conference on Alternative State and Local Policies, $4.95.

New Directions in Farm, Land and Food Policy: A Time for State and Local Action, 1979, Conference on Alternative State and Local Policies, $9.95.

New Initiatives in Farm, Land and Food Legislation: A State-by-State Guide, 1981, Conference on Alternative State and Local Policies, $4.95.

Empty Breadbasket: The Coming Challenge to America's Food Supply, 1981, Cornucopia Project of Rodale Press, $5.00.

Protecting Farmland: A Guidebook for State and Local Governments, 1981. Available from USDA, SCS, 6117 South Building, Washington, D.C. 20250. (202) 447-7443.

<u>Organizations</u>

CENTER FOR RURAL AFFAIRS, P.O. Box 405, Walthill, NE 68067 (402) 846-5428.

CONFERENCE ON ALTERNATIVE STATE AND LOCAL POLICIES, 2000 Florida Avenue, N.W., Washington, D.C. 20009 (202) 347-6030. Extensive publications on family farm issues and farmland preservation.

CORNUCOPIA PROJECT OF RODALE PRESS, 33 East Minor St., Emmaus, PA, 18049 (215) 967-5171. Information on local and regional self-sufficient food systems.

NATIONAL ASSOCIATION OF STATE DEPARTMENTS OF AGRICULTURE, 1616 H Street, N.W., Washington, D.C. 20006 (202) 628-1566. The Farmland Preservation Project does research on successful farmland preservation programs and publishes a free monthly newsletter, <u>Farmland Notes</u>.

NATIONAL FARMERS UNION, 12025 East 45th Ave., Denver, CO 80251 (303) 371-1760. General farm organization with affiliates in many states.

NATIONAL GRANGE, 1616 H Street, N.W., Washington, D.C. 20006

Prepared by Joseph Belden

Environmental Protection

<u>BACKGROUND FACTS</u>

In a March 1982 Harris poll, 80% of Republicans, 85% of Democrats, and 84% of independents said they favored stricter enforcement of air and water pollution standards.

These statistics demonstrate a widespread public awareness of the threats to personal health and welfare that pollution and misuse of natural resources pose. Public awareness has been heightened by local environmental crises such as Love Canal and Three Mile Island.

The Reagan administration has set out to roll back virtually every federal environmental program. The Reagan program of cutting federal support for environmental protection programs dramatically affects state programs. The Land, Water, and Conservation program -- the major source of state grants to develop parks -- has budgeted no more grant money for state acquisitions. Ann Gorsuch, Director of the Environmental Protection Agency, told a recent conference of southern governors that in 5 years she would "zero out" EPA's contributions to state environmental programs.

The increased activity of business political action committees, and the accompanying industrial blackmail of dislocation of jobs, threatens sound environmental programs at the federal and state level.

The landmark federal legislation on the environment has significantly contributed to the improved health and well-being of American citizens. Between 1970 and 1980, for instance, sulfer content of air dropped by 17%. This is in contrast to estimates by scientists in 1970 that sulfer content would rise by 50%.

In June 1981, <u>Newsweek</u> magazine found that 75% of Americans believe it is possible to maintain strong economic growth and high environmental standards. In September 1981, <u>A New York Times</u>/CBS poll found that two-thirds of its sample favored keeping strict air pollution laws even if some factories had to close.

<u>THE PROBLEM</u>

The needs and opportunities of an environmental agenda
extend far beyond support of federal programs. Many of the
most innovative, ambitious and successful programs can be
initiated at the state or local level. A state or community
can take steps to increase its financial stability and energy
security through aggressive programs in utility-financed energy,
conservation, bicycle facility planning, and mass transit
construction. Instead of making risky investments in high
capital energy generation facilities, utilities are beginning
to loan funds to customers to generate "conservation energy".
The energy saved through efficient insulation or generated
through solar and wind systems not only reduces the need for
huge new capital facilities; it also provides the local
community with a source of employment, and makes the community
less vulnerable to fuel cut-offs or reductions in supply.

While the public has long been concerned with keeping
air and water clean and preserving wilderness areas, the
environmental problems of the 1970s and 1980s are bringing
those concerns closer to home. Toxic waste contamination
and radiation incidents at dumpsites and reactors have made
"backyard" issues out of the environmental problems first
given national prominence at Love Canal and Three Mile Island.

At the same time, the significant progress achieved in
cleaning up traditional sources of air and water pollution
has demonstrated our ability to solve pollution problems
without staggering economic consequences. This progress has
not only created new support for environmental programs
among citizens who recognize the improvement in their local
rivers or local air quality; it has also created new pollution
control industries that benefit from environmental programs.

President Reagan has initiated polices under the guise
of regulatory relief for business that would roll back or
eliminate virtually every federal environmental program in
existence. Currently, grassroots environmental groups are
investigating the local effects of the Reagan policies on
their states and communities. This research amply demonstrates
that the well-publicized policies of Interior Secretary
James Watt and Environmental Protection Agency Administrator
Ann Gorsuch are only the tip of the federal government's
anti-environmental iceberg. This abandonment of the federal
commitment to environmental programs makes state and local
environmental leadership crucial.

In tandem with the Reagan policies, the explosive growth of business political action committees and industrial "job blackmail" has brought environmental policies directly into the partisan political arena. Contributions from polluting industries to political candidates clearly have had an effect upon congressionial responses to environmental problems. In many localities where prevailing economic difficulties have threatened the continued operation of major industrial facilities, corporations have used the threat of job loss as a club with which to beat back needed environmental regulations.

Increasingly, labor unions and environmentalists are working together to secure a healthy workplace and community, together with economic stability and prosperity. The OSHA/Environmental Network is a nationwide coalition of labor unions and environmental organizations that have joined forces on such issues of common concern as occupational safety and health, clean air legislation, worker and community right-to-know legislation, and clean water legislation. Together, these groups can make a more accurate assessment of real economic costs of regulation and can reveal the often spurious nature of the corporate link between environmental regulations and plant closures.

Because of the retreat in federal programs, state support for environmental programs is more crucial than ever. States need to increase their funding for pollution control enforcement as the federal EPA under Administrator Gorsuch cuts its own budget and engages in wasteful and paralyzing reorganization each year.

State enforcement of mine safety and workplace health regulation must also replace federal programs crippled by Secretary Watt and OSHA Administrator Thorne Auchter. As federal clean air regulations come under attack, state leadership is needed to support the automobile inspection and maintenance programs. These regulations have not only proved effective in reducing urban air pollution; they also have proved to be popular with motorists who find that the routine maintenance required actually saves them money at the fuel pump.

In addition to preserving and enforcing existing federal programs, state leaders must be vigilant to prevent their enforcement of stricter state regulations from being preempted by the federal government. For example, several attempts have been made in Congress this year to prevent California from enforcing stricter clean air provisions.

<u>WHAT STATES CAN DO</u>

<u>Enforcing Anti-Pollution Laws</u>

° States should increase funding and staffing for enforcement
  and administration of pollution control programs. Almost
  every state shares the responsibilities with federal EPA.
  Such increases will help compensate for federal budget
  cuts and administration policies that will increasingly
  make state government the only defense against pollution.

<u>Developing Local Energy Security</u>

° States should enact legislation to encourage utility investment in conservation development. Through loans to utility
  customers, insulation, weatherization, solar hot water and
  domestic and commercial heat can be achieved, with local
  businesses and worker receiving the financial benefit of
  community investment.

<u>Develop a Conserving Transportation System</u>

° States should "trade in" uncompleted segments of interstate
  highways for funds that can be used for mass transit and
  highway maintenance purposes.

° States should enact heavy truck weight distance taxes
  rather than increase regressive gasoline taxes. Trucks
  are responsible for most highway damage according to
  current federal and state cost allocation studies.

<u>Conserving Our Resources</u>

° States should establish soil conservation programs, which
  are desperately needed to reduce the critical losses of
  topsoil caused by modern agricultural practices.

° States should establish programs for organic farm research
  to provide an economic alternative to the current systems
  that are bankrupting family farms throughout the nation.

° States should act to acquire critical habitats and tracts
  for greenline parks and wild area protection. In areas
  near cities where outright acquisition may be financially
  impossible environmentally sensitve regional zoning can be
  very effective.

° States should enact bottle and can deposit laws which have
  proven effective in nine states and have recently been
  approved in New York State.

<u>FOR FURTHER INFORMATION</u>

<u>Publications</u>

Ronald Reagan and the American Environment, published by
Friends of the Earth Books, 1045 Sansome St., San Francisco,
CA 94111, $6.95. A critique prepared by ten national envi-
ronmental groups of Reagan environmental policies.

Progress as if Survival Mattered, edited by Hugh Nash,
Friends of the Earth Books, 1045 Sansome St., San Francisco,
CA, 94111, $14.95. A compendium of articles on the full
range of environmental problems and opportunites.

Fear At Work: Job Blackmail, Labor and the Environment,
by Richard Kazis and Richard Grossman, available from
Environmentalists for Full Employment, 1536 16th St., N.W.,
Washington, D.C., 20036, $9.95. An expose of corporate
campaigns to gut workplace and environmental regulations by
using the promise of jobs and the threat of unemployment to
blackmail workers and communities.

The Green Vote Handbook, available from the Sierra Club,
530 Bush St., San Francisco, CA, 94108. Useful introduction
for environmentalists in politics.

<u>Organizations</u>

FRIENDS OF THE EARTH, 530 7th St., S.E., Washington, D.C.,
20003 (202) 543-4312. Pete Lafen, Transportation Counsel.
An environmental group working on a wide range of issues.

ENVIRONMENTAL ACTION, 1346 Connecticut Ave., N.W.,Suite 731,
Washington, D.C., 20036 (202) 833-1845. Maintains a national
clearinghouse for information on bottle bill legislation in
state legislatures and municipal governments.

THE WILDERNESS SOCIETY, 1901 Pennsylvania Ave., N.W.,
Washington, D.C. (202) 828-6600.

THE OSHA/ENVIRONMENT NETWORK, 815 16th St., N.W., Room 301,
Washington, D.C., 20006, (202) 842-7820. Pam Woywod, Director.
The national headquarters of network organizations and leaders
in worker health and community safety initiatives throughout
the country.

THE LEAGUE OF CONSERVATION VOTERS, 317 Pennsylvania Ave.,
S.E., Washington, D.C., 20003 (202) 547-7200. Marion Edey,
Director. The oldest and largest environmental political
action committee and can provide information on local political
activites.

Prepared by Peter Lafen

Nuclear Energy

<u>BACKGROUND FACTS</u>

In the early 1950s, the Atoms for Peace program portrayed atomic energy as a means of assuring abundant energy forever with little or no risk.

According to early proponents, electricity produced by atomic power plants would be "too cheap to meter." Thirty years later, that optimism appears as a parody of reality. Today, utilities are nearly bankrupt in many areas of the country because they committed themselves to nuclear reactors.

The amount of highly radioactive nuclear waste grows constantly with no solution in sight, and profoundly serious issues have arisen concerning the safety of nuclear power.

The bright future of nuclear power began to unravel in the mid-1970s. Costs escalated rapidly, to the point that prominent analysts argued that even coal-fired plants, with their high fuel costs, were more economical than nuclear power.

Large nuclear reactors were predicted to be capable of actually delivering only about 57% of their possible electric output. By the early 1980's, nuclear plants predicted to cost $900 million or less had risen in cost to $4 billion, with no maximum in sight.

More important than costs, however, were safety concerns. In 1975, a serious fire occurred at the Browns Ferry facility in Alabama. In 1976, a Nuclear Regulatory Commission (NRC) staff member with broad responsibilities over several reactors, and three members of the General Electric nuclear program resigned in protest over inadequate safety precautions. In 1979, an accident occurred at Unit 2 of the Three Mile Island facility in Pennsylvania. To date, tens of thousands of people had to be evacuated from the area.

Three Mile Island might have been a turning point, spurring stricter safety measures and greater protection. Instead, there was a backlash that ultimately resulted in intense pressures to grant reactor licenses without delay, and the important safety lessons of the accident have been largely ignored.

While public attention has focused on the reactor safety issue, the long-term problem of nuclear waste remains unresolved. The federal government is confident that a disposal repository will be available soon, but it has had the same confidence for at least a decade.

The use of nuclear reactors poses three fundamental problems: reactor safety, radioactive waste management and disposal, and grossly excessive cost. To date, the role of the states in any of these issues has been severely limited, partly by federal preemption, and partly by the failure of state utility regulatory commissions to require sound financial planning by nuclear utilities.

Reactor safety is clearly beyond the bounds of state authority in terms of technical requirements. Under the Atomic Energy Act the Nuclear Regulatory Commission has complete authority in that area. However, states have an important role in emergency planning for possible reactor accidents.

State activity is similarly restricted with respect to radioactive waste management and disposal, although pending federal legislation may create a formal advisory role. Generally, the area for explicit state activity is that of considerations not directly related to reactor safety. States can affect safety issues indirectly by careful attention to costs, economic impacts, and whether a nuclear plant should be constructed at all.

Ultimately the problem of nuclear energy is the problem of how best to meet the nation's energy needs in both the shortand the long-term. It is here that cost becomes extremely important, and here is where states can take the lead. The massive amounts of capital committed to nuclear power stretched utilities to the breaking point. They have also diverted essential resources from the development of less costly, less capital-intensive, more efficient, and safer means of providing energy.

<u>State Responses</u> Efforts in Congress and elsewhere at the federal level to bring rationality to the nuclear issue have been thwarted by the Reagan administration's abdication of energy policy and by the nuclear industry's political influence in Congress.

The states have been far more creative and sensitive to the serious problems of nuclear power. The primary example is California, which enacted a provision that would ban new nuclear reactors until a solution has been found for the disposal of nuclear wastes. California has thus far avoided federal preemption in this area by basing its legislative concern on the likely economic impact of a failure to solve the waste problem rather than on nuclear safety issues. California's approach was upheld by a U.S. Court of Appeals, although the Supreme Court has recently agreed to hear the nuclear industry appeal. Other states have already followed California's lead.

The primary tool of state action should be the state regulatory commission, which usually has the authority to regulate expenditures by state utilities, thereby controlling the size and type of generating plants. Pennsylvania recently exercised that authority by effectively cancelling one of the units of the Limerick plant, and the New Hampshire Public Utilities Commission is closely scrutinizing Unit 2 of the Seabrook facility and may order significant delay or cancellation.

Similarly, those states that refuse to grant rate increases to pay for Construction Work in Progress (CWIP) force the utilities to use their own money to fund nuclear construction. Since nuclear plants are generally perceived as bad investments, this should effectively halt nuclear construction in a state where it occurs.

Another area where serious state action should be fruitful is emergency planning. All nuclear reactors are required to have emergency plans that provide for protection, including evacuation, up to at least 10 miles from the reactors. In many cases, such planning has been nothing more than a sham, with no real assurances that traffic estimates and evacuation times are reasonably correct. States should insist on the use of independent consultants with no ties to the nuclear industry and demand that the needs and interests of localities be addressed in full.

State programs to conserve energy, manage peak loads, encourage conservation and promote alternative energy sources will probably have more impact than any other policies in minimizing the use of nuclear power. With no real need, nuclear reactors cannot be justified on economic grounds.

The major argument that is used in favor of nuclear power is that it supplies an essential energy resource and frees this nation from oil dependence. If that were true, it would doubtless be reflected in the marketplace to some extent; but it is not. There have been no new reactor orders since well before Three Mile Island, and plants are constantly being cancelled by utilities or halted for lack of funds through regulatory or legislative action.

In fact, nuclear energy provides a relatively small percentage (11%) of only one type of energy -- electricity -- which constitutes a relatively small proportion of our total energy use. Since only about 9% of U.S. electricity is generated with oil, even complete replacement of that amount with nuclear power would have little effect. All of America's nuclear reactors could be replaced by a major conservation effort conducted in conjunction with intensive development of alternative energy sources.

<u>WHAT STATES CAN DO</u>

<u>Nuclear Waste</u>

° States should enact legislation similar to California's to
  put a moratorium on the construction of new nuclear reactors,
  and perhaps even the operation of existing reactors until a
  firm solution to the nuclear waste disposal problem has been
  found.

° States should explore their own lands to determine whether
  any potential disposal sites for radioactive wastes exist
  within their boundaries.

° States should participate to the fullest extent in any
  mechanism established by federal legislation for state
  involvement in waste repository decisions.

<u>Controlling the Generation Mix and Minimizing Costs</u>

° States should require the use of independent consultants to
  evaluate utility projections and to develop independent
  cost and need projections. These consultants can be paid
  through levies against the utilities.

° States should pass legislation banning the use of Construction Work in Progress (CWIP) payments.

° States should establish and require utilities to establish
  programs to promote energy conservation, load management,
  cogeneration, and the use of alternative energy sources.

° States should clearly establish that unneeded plants will
  not be allowed in the utilities' rate bases.

<u>Nuclear Safety</u>

° States should be closely involved in the emergency planning
  process for reactors within their borders or near their
  borders and should demand independent consultants and accurate
  and realistic assumptions.

° States should participate in licensing hearings and should
  provide substantial resources to evaluate and refute the
  positions taken by the utilities and the NRC staff.

° States should establish special offices to represent the
  public or should require utilities to contribute to a special
  fund to pay for participation by citizen groups in NRC
  licensing hearings and in state rate and other regulatory
  proceedings.

FOR FURTHER INFORMATION

Publications

Power Plant Cost Escalation: Nuclear and Coal Capital Costs, and Economics, Charles Komanoff, Komanoff Energy Associates, New York, 1981. The best information available on the costs of nuclear construction.

Accidents Will Happen: The Case Against Nuclear Power, Lee Stephenson and George R. Zachar, Eds., The Environmental Action Foundation, Harper & Row, 1979. Useful introductory material on the full range of nuclear issues.

Report of the President's Commission on the Accident at Three Mile Island, the Need for Change: the Legacy of TMI, U.S. Government Printing Office, October 1979. A thorough examination and discussion of the TMI accident, including an evaluation of the industry and NRC failures that contributed to it.

Radioactive Waste: Politics, Technology and Risk, Ronnie D. Lipshutz, published for the Union of Concerned Scientists by Ballinger Publishing Co., 1980. A thorough discussion of the issue of radioactive waste management and disposal, with a description of the elements required for a successful program.

Organizations

UNION OF CONCERNED SCIENTISTS, 1346 Connecticut Avenue, N.W., Washington, D.C. 20036 (202) 296-5600. A technically-oriented organization with knowledge of all areas and particular expertise in nuclear safety issues.

ENVIRONMENTAL ACTION and ENVIRONMENTAL ACTION FOUNDATION, 1346 Conn. Ave., N.W., Washington, D.C. 20036 (202) 833-1845 and 659-1130. Closely related organizations with information on all issues and particular strengths in the areas of costs and rate impacts of nuclear power and alternative energy sources.

NUCLEAR INFORMATION AND RESOURCE CENTER, 1346 Connecticut Ave., N.W., Washington, D.C. 20036 (202) 296-7552. A clearing-house for nuclear information.

CRITICAL MASS ENERGY PROJECT, 215 Pennsylvania Ave., S.E., Washington, D.C. 20003 (202) 546-4790. An organization concerned with all aspects of nuclear issues.

Prepared by William Jordan.

Solar and Energy Conservation

<u>BACKGROUND FACTS</u>

Two nationwide polls conducted during the 1980 Presidential campaign -- one by Gallup, the other by Roper and Cantril -- revealed that more Americans want to see renewable energy used to meet United States energy demand than any other energy option.

This popular support should come as no surprise. Used wisely, power from the sun, wind, falling water, and plants is gentle to the environment. They are cheaper -- and pose fewer safety risks -- than the fossil fuel and nuclear alternatives.

After two major oil price shocks, energy conservation has also become a widely used and accepted part of the American economy. The amount of energy needed to produce a dollar of GNP has decreased by about six percent since 1978 and American buildings, industries, and vehicles are approximately 18 per cent more efficient today than they were in 1973.

Still tiny by fossil energy industry standards, the solar and conservation industries have nevertheless grown dramatically in the past four years. For example, the number of passive solar homes, in which the building itself functions as a solar collector, has increased from approximately 500 in 1977 to almost 80,000 in 1982. National alcohol fuel capacity will increase from 1.5 million gallons to 1978 to 400 million gallons by late 1982.

In 1980, sales for active solar systems, passive solar designs, photovoltaics, wind energy machines, biomass conversion, hydroelectric facilities, and geothermal systems reached $4.5 billion.

U.S. spending for energy conservation rose from less than $2 billion in 1978 to $8.7 billion in 1985 and will reach $50 billion in 1990, according to <u>Business Week</u>.

A variety of government and university studies confirm that conservation and solar measures are our nation's wisest and most economic energy alternatives. According to <u>A New Prosperity</u>, the U.S. can increase productivity and reduce energy needs by 25 percent simply by increasing the efficiency of our energy use. Of the remaining demand in the year 2000, 20 to 30 percent could be met by renewable resources.

Although the temporary oil surplus has fortunately eliminated gas lines and slightly reduced energy prices, energy
remains a major concern for the United States. Despite reduced
oil imports, the U.S. still spent almost $70 billion for for-
eign oil in 1981. The resulting poor balance-of-payments
and inflation have been key sources of our economic problems.
Moreover, this country's oil supply lines from the Middle
East remain militarily vulnerable.

From an environmental perspective our conventional power
plants continue to produce acid rain, carbon dioxide, and
radioactive wastes. Some new energy plans call for increased
stripping of the land for coal production and diversion of the
West's precious water resources.

Unfortunately, The Reagan administration has developed
a dangerous, costly, and hypocritical energy policy. If the
White House gets its way, the energy conservation budget
will be slashed by 97 percent, and the solar budget by 87
percent. The Solar and Conservation Bank will be destroyed.
State energy assistance and weatherization programs for
low-income people will be eliminated. Appliance labeling,
energy information programs, and energy audits will be for-
gotten. And business energy tax credits will be repealed.

But while President Reagan uses free enterprise rhetoric
to justify solar and conservation reductions, he has increased
the 1982 nuclear budget by 36 percent; maintained synthetic
fuel subsidies; and granted $12 billion of new tax benefits
to the oil companies. If the White House gets its way, we
will spend more on the military marching bands than on all
solar and conservation efforts combined.

The Reagan plan is also bad for businesses. Both Japan
and France now spend more per capita than the United States
on solar energy development, and recent studies suggest tht
foreign firms will soon capture the lucrative photovoltaics
market, largely because the administration has abandoned the
solar cell program.

But some of the most serious impacts of the Reagan energy
plan affect individuals and families. By destroying the
weatherization programs and the Solar and Conservation Bank,
the Administration is hurting low-income people and hindering
their efforts to become energy self-reliant. Without financing
assistance, the poor cannot afford the up-front costs of
conservation and solar improvements, despite the long-term
economic benefits. It is a national disgrace that an esti-

mated 1.5 million American homes went without heat or lights this winter, and hundreds died from hypothermia, largely because they could not afford energy.

Although energy problems are national in scope, they vary within each state. But many states and communities are exporting large amounts of money from their areas for energy. Those funds are not recycled within the local economy.

Until recently, few states developed comprehensive energy plans. Confused by the national and international forces affecting energy supply and prices, most state legislatures have approved only patchwork measures to use their energy more efficiently and to develop local renewable resources.

It is hard to directly attack motherhood, apple pie, or solar energy. But renewable energy opponents contend that solar technologies are "exotic" fantasies that cannot produce useful energy until the 21st century. These critics ignore the fact that renewable energy sources (primarily hydroelectric dams and the burning of wood) supply more total energy than do all the nation's nuclear reactors. Even the Harvard Business School projects solar technologies can soon supply more power than natural gas or coal and nuclear power combined.

Conservation critics maintain that the nation needs more energy to fuel economic growth. But conservation means meeting our needs for lighting, warmth, mobility, and industrial process energy in the most economic and efficient manner possible. Recent economic measures confirm this point. Between 1973 and 1980, U.S. energy consumption rose by a total of only 2 percent. Over this same period, real Gross National Product -- corrected for inflation --- rose by 18 percent. Thus, almost 90 percent of the economic growth during these eight years was supported through increases in national energy productivity and only 10 percent through the introduction of additional energy sources.

Solar and conservation critics also maintain that <u>the government</u> should not promote alternative energy development because the free market should be allowed to operate. Unfortunately, the energy market is anything but free. According to Battelle Institute, the federal government has given more than $225 billion in subsidies to the coal, oil, and nuclear power industries. Some $14 billion in tax benefits are still given annually to these firms. For solar and conservation measures to receive a fair shake, <u>either all energy subsidies must be eliminated</u> or <u>a balanced energy program must be developed.</u>

<u>WHAT STATES CAN DO</u>

The two major barriers to solar and conservation development are the lack of consumer education and the lack of financing.

<u>Financing</u>

° States should enact residential and business tax credits to stimulate energy conservation and for the use of solar and other renewable energy sources.

° States should develop programs that would provide low interest loans to homeowners, multi-family buildings, and businesses for energy conservation or for renewable energy improvements, either from direct government funds or through utility or commercial bank loans.

° States with severance taxes should use a percentage of their funds to fund energy development projects aimed at reducing the state's reliance on non-renewable energy.

° States should impose a surcharge on utilities to finance independent corporations to fund renewable energy and conservation projects throughout the state.

° States should increase the maximum loan limit to veterans for mortgages or homes equipped with renewable energy devices.

° States should stimulate alcohol fuels development by establishing tax credits for state residents who modify vehicles to use pure alcohol, waive the state sales tax on gasoline, provide grants and low-interest loans for small-scale alcohol production, and fund an extensive research program to identify new alcohol feedstocks.

<u>Public Education</u>

° States should provide information and/or training on solar and energy conservation options.

° States should initiate small grants programs for individuals who want to build conservation and renewable energy devices to offset high energy costs.

<u>FOR FURTHER INFORMATION</u>

<u>Publications</u>

A New Prosperity: Building A Sustainable Energy Future,
The Solar Energy Research Institute Solar/Conservation Study,
1982. Available for $20.95 from Brick House Publishing, 34
Essex St., Andover, MA 01810. The most comprehensive review
of the potential for solar and conservation measures.

Shining Examples: Model Projects Using Renewable Resources,
Center for Renewable Resources, 1980. Available for $6.95
from the Center for Renewable Resources, Publications
Department, 641 S. Pickett St., Alexandria, VA, 22304.
Features 150 practical and creative community-based programs
using conservation and renewable energy measures.

State and Local Solar Energy Policy: Meeting Low Income
Needs, 1981. Available for $4.95 from the Conference on Al-
ternative State and Local Policies.

Energy Conservation and the Poor: Strategies for State
and Local Governments, 1982. Available for $4.95 from the
Conference on Alternative State and Local Policies.

New Initiatives in Energy Legislation: A State-by-State
Guide, 1981-1982, 1981. Available for $5.95 from the Conference
on Alternative State and Local Policies.

<u>Organizations</u>

CONFERENCE ON ALTERNATIVE STATE AND LOCAL POLICIES, 2000
Florida Ave., N.W., Washington, D.C. 20036 (202) 387-6030.
Lee Webb, Director. Has available a catalogue of solar and
energy conservation publications.

ENERGY CONSERVATION COALITION, 1725 Eye St., N.W., Washington,
D.C. 20006 (202) 466-5045. Farwell Smith or David Moulton.

INSTITUTE FOR LOCAL SELF-RELIANCE, 1717 18th St., N.W.,
Washington, D.C. 20009 (202) 232-4108. David Morris, Director.

NATIONAL CENTER FOR APPROPRIATE TECHNOLOGY, Box 3838, Butte,
MT, 59701 (406) 494-4572. Joe Sedlack, Director.

SOLAR LOBBY and the CENTER FOR RENEWABLE RESOURCES, 1001
Connecticut Ave., N.W., Washington, D.C. 20036 (202) 466-
6350. Richard Munson, Director.

Prepared by Richard Munson

Toxics

<u>BACKGROUND FACTS</u>

Toxic substances are present throughout our environment.
"The entire population of the nation, and indeed the world,
carries some body burden of one or several" toxins, according
to a Library of Congress survey of chemical contamination.

More than 30,000 chemicals are in general commercial use
and more than 1,000 new chemicals are developed annually. Yet
only a few hundred of these chemicals are tested each year to
determine whether they may be carcinogenic (cancer causing),
mutagenic (causing genetic damage to the cells), teratogenic
(causing damage to the developing fetus) or may result in other
long-term adverse health effects.

No one can escape exposure to potentially hazardous
chemicals:

° Millions of workers are exposed to toxic substances in the
  workplace. Occupational exposure to these substances
  account for between 300,000 and 600,000 illnesses and
  deaths each year (or about half of all occupational illnesses and deaths).

° Consumers are exposed through produce laden with pesticide
  residues, through insulation emitting carcinogenic formalde-
  hyde fumes and through hundreds of other products containing
  such substances as asbestos, phenols, benzene and the like.

° The four billion tons of chemicals carried each year by
  road, rail and waterway pose risks to communities of every
  size.

° Everyone is at risk from improper disposal of the estimated
  66 to 88 billion pounds of hazardous waste generated each
  year. There are between 32,000 and 50,000 sites where
  such waste has been disposed. At least 2,000 of these
  sites pose significant environmental/ health dangers and
  warrant quick remedial action. Hazardous waste particularly
  threatens ground water. About 50 per cent of all Americans
  rely on ground water for drinking water. Millions of
  citizens nationwide have had their municipal and private
  wells closed due to chemical contamination.

<u>THE PROBLEM</u>

Mention the word "toxics," and the first thing that comes to an American's mind is "Love Canal." That community in up-state New York, where the legacy of years of hazardous waste dumping forced hundreds of families from their homes forever, is an important national symbol. However, toxics, and the threat from toxics is much bigger than Love Canal. Toxics problems begin with the manufacture of hazardous substances and continues through distribution, use and eventual disposal of those substances. Toxics are a widely-based, long-term problem. Toxics control requires a broad, integrated and long-range approach.

Although the routes of toxic exposure are almost limitless, it is often difficult to recognize the immediate effects of exposure. Some victims, such as small children, may experience immediate health problems. But others exposed to toxic substances may not suffer health effects until many years after initial exposure. As many as 30 years may pass before the onset of cancer, leukemia or other health problems caused by toxic exposure.

In some instances, health effects may even skip a generation. This latency period can make it difficult to prove the cause-and-effect connection between toxic exposure and disease and so make it difficult to enact strong toxic controlling laws now.

At least ten major federal laws cover various aspects of toxics control. Perhaps most important of these laws are the Toxic Substances Control Act (TSCA), the Occupational Safety and Health Act (OSHA), the Federal Insecticide, Fungicide and Rodenticide Act (FIFRA) and the Resource Conservation and Recovery Act (RCRA). TSCA covers the testing of new chemicals and existing chemicals; OSHA covers workplace hazards; FIFRA covers the sale and use of pesticides and RCRA calls for "cradle to grave" regulation of all wastes, including hazardous waste. In addition, the Comprehensive Environmental Response, Compensation and Liability Act (CERCLA) -- for which states must provide matching funds -- better known as Superfund, provides for the clean up of a limited number (400 sites) of abandoned hazardous waste dumps.

This formidable array of federal laws, however, has been undercut by massive budget and manpower cuts. In particular, the Environmental Protection Agency (EPA), with primary responsibility for TSCA, FIFRA, RCRA and Superfund, has had its budget and workforce halved just as its workload has doubled. Worse yet, EPA seems to have abandoned its mandated objective of aggressively protecting the environment and public health.

EPA's backpedalling has not gone unnoticed. Even the industry journal <u>Chemical Week</u> admits that the federal government seems to be abandoning its environmental protection role: "No one pretends that market forces will protect the environment...Without an effective EPA, industry's contribution to pollution, which has been diminishing, is bound to grow again."

And state officials have noted the impact of an eviscerated EPA. James K. Hambright, president of the State and Territorial Air Pollution Program Administrators, wrote in a letter to Rep. Toby Moffett (D-CT) that "EPA's inexplicable rush to cut its throat will do the same to us...State programs need the technical support that EPA has provided in standard setting and strategy development. We must also have the backup of federal enforcement to ensure compliance with our regulations. Without strong EPA programs...state programs will be largely ineffective."

Aggressive and effective state actions to control toxics need strong federal toxic control programs. Federal programs, in addition to technical and enforcement support, provide overall standards for state, county, and municipal efforts. Without federal standards, state and local toxic control can fall victim to destructive and "beggar thy neighbor" competition between the states or localities. As the vice president of one major hazardous waste management firm noted: "Unfortunately, it is clear that not all states will enact comprehensive preventive legislation if left to their own devices -- particularly if influenced by continued relaxation of federal guidelines. This relaxation means that increased quantities of hazardous waste will be landfilled in those states which have the weakest regulations and are, therefore, the least equipped to handle the hazardous waste problems which will arise in later years."

Manufacturing Hazards

° States should pass legislation that would force industry to
reduce the amount of hazardous waste generated during production through such means as materials recovery, recycling,
and manufacturing process changes. Kentucky, Kansas,
Maine, Missouri, Tennessee and Indiana levy fees against
the generators of hazardous waste. Illinois offers tax-exempt,
low interest bonds for construction of facilities engaged
in "reducing, controlling or preventing pollution...(or
attempting to) reduce the volume or composition of hazardous
waste."

Protecting Workers and the Community

° States should pass right-to-know legislation that gives
workers and community residents the right to know the
identity and potential dangers of hazardous chemicals
used, stored or produced at local industrial firms. Right-
to-know laws in California, New Jersey, Michigan, Massachusetts, Maine, New York, Wisconsin and West Virginia grant
this right, though only to workers.

Protecting Against Toxic Products

° States should pass legislation that will keep potentially
harzardous products from entering the marketplace. Examples
include urea-formaldehyde foam insulation, which emits
noxious and potentially carcinogenic fumess. Massachusetts
has enacted legislation banning such insulation.

Hazardous Waste Disposal

° States should pass legislation requiring that the safest
and most effective technologies are being used to manage
those wastes which cannot be reduced or recycled. California
has established a program that not only bans land disposal
of certain highly toxic wastes but also provides industry
with technical assistance to find alternative disposal and
reduction techniques.

Hazardous Waste Clean Up

° States should establish superfunds to clean up hazardous
waste dumps. Several states, including New Jersey, New
York, Connecticut and California have passed state superfund
legislation. Money for these funds comes in part from a
tax levied against either generators or disposers of
hazardous waste.

<u>FOR FURTHER INFORMATION</u>

<u>Publications</u>

Right to Know Information Packet Vol. I & II, $7 per pack-
et business/$3.50 per packet other; <u>Hazardous Materials Trans-</u>
<u>portation Info Packet</u>, $7 business/3.50 other; <u>Pesticide</u>
<u>Information Packet</u>, $6 business/ $3 other. These and other
packets on toxics are available from the Waste and Toxic Substances Project of the Environmental Action Foundation.

<u>Waste and Toxic Substances Resource Guide</u>, $2.00, Waste and
Toxic Substances Project of the Environmental Action Foundation.

<u>Training Materials on Toxic Substances</u>, an organizing
handbook and resource guide. Available for $15.00 from the
Sierra Club, 530 Bush St., San Francisco, CA, 94108.

<u>Exposure</u>, national monthly news journal on waste and toxic
issues. Available from Waste and Toxic Substances Project of
Environmental Action Foundation: $25 regular, $15 citizen group,
$10 low-income or senior citizen, $50 business per annual
subscription.

<u>Organizations</u>

ENVIRONMENTAL ACTION FOUNDATION, Waste and Toxic Substances
Project, 724 Dupont Circle Building, Washington, D.C. 20036
(202) 296-7570. Operates national information clearinghouse
on waste and toxic issues and publishes the monthly newsletter <u>Exposure</u>.

ENVIRONMENTAL DEFENSE FUND, 1525 18th St., N.W., Washington,
D.C. 20036 (202) 833-1484. Litigates on waste and toxics
issues and does technical research.

CENTER FOR OCCUPATIONAL HAZARDS, 5 Beekman St., New York, NY
10038 (212) 227-6220. Operates clearinghouse on occupational
hazard issues.

NATIONAL COALITION AGAINST THE MISUSE OF PESTICIDES, 530 7th
St., S.E., Washington, D.C. 20003 (202) 543-4313, Jay Feldman.

CITIZENS CLEARINGHOUSE FOR HAZARDOUS WASTES, P.O. Box 1097,
Arlington, VA 22207 (703) 532-6816.

FRIENDS OF THE EARTH, 124 Spear St., San Francisco,CA 94105
(405) 495-4770. Active on variety of toxic issues, particularly
pesticides.

Prepared by James Lewis.

Water and Sewers

BACKGROUND FACTS

The coming water crisis -- which has already arrived in several areas of the country -- is likely to have an impact equal to or greater than that of last decade's energy crisis. Many states have felt the effects of water and sewage management problems in terms of higher costs for water and sewage services, reduced opportunities for economic growth, and threats to public health.

California, Connecticut, New Jersey and many other states have been hit with severe water shortages, which in many areas are exacerbated by toxic contamination. Underground water supplies across the country are being drained.

Water and sewer systems are reaching the end of their design life in many of the nation's older cities. Cities and states will have to make repairs and replacements costing tens of billions of dollars. Repairing the hemorrhaging of New York City's 6,000 miles of sewers will cost billions. The federal government, whose policies more often promote the construction of new projects than the repair of existing systems, is unlikely to offer much assistance.

Many states' sewage policies discourage the use of treatment technologies that recycle water and wastes and use less energy -- systems that are especially appropriate and affordable. Traditional techniques have other high costs, including the unwanted, harmful development and needless loss of agricultural land and water.

Dangerous chemicals have contaminated drinking water and the food chain. Many states warn residents against eating fish from waters contaminated by chemical effluvia, including those of the Great Lakes, and the Hudson and James Rivers. Water supplies in 29 percent of U.S. towns are contaminated with industrial chemicals, according to a recent EPA report.

The runoff of soil and pesticides from agricultural areas and of metals and toxic organic materials from cities damages water quality throughout the country. States are on their own in finding solutions to these problems.

Workers at sewage treatment plants, hazardous waste and other environmental facilities often lack the training to manage sophisticated processes. Billions have been wasted constructing facilities which do not produce clean water or effective waste management because of improper operation and maintenance.

<u>THE PROBLEM</u>

While water problems vary from place to place, most fit
into one or more of the following patterns:

<u>Money</u>: Massive sums of money are needed for municipal
water and sewage treatment, infrastructure repair and replacement, the cleanup of toxic wastes, and enforcement activities.
The bill for tackling these problems is likely to be charged,
in large part, to state governments. Federal budget cuts have
translated into reduced efforts in the pollution control field.
Funding for the municipal wastewater treatment construction
grants program, for example, has been cut by more than a third.

Funding for federal enforcement of major water protection
laws has also been sharply cut, leaving this difficult task to
the states. The Reagan Administration's "New Federalism" program will mean that water quality programs will be forced to
compete with a host of other worthy social programs. The
country's economic woes compound the problem, especially in
many parts of the Midwest and Northeast where the flight of
capital is most severe.

States can begin to seek alternate sources of money to
replace the traditional routes. Pension funds, cooperative
funding, lease-back arrangements, mixed private-public ventures,
revolving loan funds, and a variety of ways to make scarce
public monies leverage larger sums of private capital are among
the policies that merit exploration.

Some control technologies are themselves revenue producing.
Hagerstown, Maryland is using its wastewater to grow trees
which will yield alcohol fuel.

Beyond deciding what kinds of projects to fund, states
and communities face hard decisions over where to target
their public dollars and the private dollars that follow.
Too often in the past, much of the money has assisted new
suburban areas -- a policy promoted by powerful construction,
land, banking and development interests -- leaving less for
older central city areas most in need of pollution clean-up
and financial help. More conscious criteria are needed for
capital allocation to achieve the most cost-effective results
and to guard against this "sewer redlining". Needed too are
better mechanisms to permit concerned citizen groups to have
their voices heard and needs met in debates over where the
money goes.

<u>High Tech vs. Appropriate Technology</u>: Traditional re-
sponses to water problems have often included expensive engineering solutions that failed to adequately recognize
resource limits. Building new sewage treatment plants, dams

to create a new water supply, and water diversion projects
often cost more and accomplish less than plugging leaky
sewers, preventing pollution, protecting groundwater recharge
areas and conserving water in a myriad of other ways.

State policies are needed which aggressively encourage
conservation, including permitting or even requiring water
utilities to front the cost of water conservation devices for
their customers and get the payback as part of the water bill
process. Public grants and credit guarantees for a variety
of activities, including new housing and building construction,
can be conditioned on the maximum use of conservation techniques. In addition to saving dollars and water, appropriate
technologies also create jobs.

<u>Regulations</u>: The problem of hazardous waste cleanup is
economic, not technological. Companies like to skimp on clean-
up costs, arguing that the economy is better served when their
costs are less and their profits larger. This approach ignores costs to the communities in property and health damage.
Moreover, it ignores the direct economic benefits -- including
cleanup jobs, the commitment to continued operation that
accompanies a polluter's investment in control technology, and
the recapture of valuable waste products currently thrown away
-- that come with pollution controls.

Stronger law enforcement is one state weapon in the battle
against toxic violence. Strict inspection and enforcement of
dumping laws (financed by surcharges on industries generating
potentially hazardous wastes) and broad right-to-know laws
(informing workers and community residents of the chemicals
they are exposed to) encourage more careful management.

<u>Pricing</u>: Distorted pricing policies which reward waste
are at the root of many pollution and shortage problems.
Changing to water "lifeline" rates (or other rate structures
which charge large users more) help protect poor and middle-
income people, promote conservation, and raise more revenue
from big users to finance safety improvements. It is especially
important that large commercial users pay their fair share for
water and sewer services. Pollution taxes -- fees based on the
amount of waste discharged -- are no substitute for standards
or prohibitions where dangerous toxics are concerned. But if
combined with regulations, they could give a strong economic
incentive for pollution control and may generate substantial
revenue for the state as well.

<u>WHAT STATES CAN DO</u>

<u>Encouraging Better Use of Water</u>

° States should enact legislation to encourage more efficient
  uses of water. Legislation should encourage water-saving
  irrigation techniques, changes in plumbing codes to permit
  the use of water conservation devices, and the establishment
  of rate structures that promote conservation, such as
  "lifeline" rates. California and New Jersey have created
  aggressive water conservation programs.

° States should encourage the use of sewage treatment techniques that use less energy and recycle water and wastes. In
  many states, changes in sanitary codes are necessary to encourage these less costly techniques. New York, California
  and other states have passed legislation allowing creation
  of on-site wastewater districts. These districts provide
  rural areas with more flexible institutions to construct and
  manage on-site sewage treatment systems, like septic tanks.
  Michigan has passed a law to encourage the recycling of
  graywater (wastewater from showers and sinks).

° States should adopt policies to encourage recycling and
  reuse of wastewater and by-products of the treatment process.
  Preventing contamination by toxic substances is essential to
  promoting safe recycling of domestic wastewater. Colorado
  and other states have given priority to sewage treatment
  projects that recycle wastes.

<u>Protecting Water Supplies</u>

° States should map aquifer recharge areas and enact legislation to prevent development where the quality or quantity
  of underground water resources might be adversely affected.
  New York and Connecticut are examples of states that have
  begun to map their aquifers.

° States should limit the levels of or ban phosphates. Phosphate bans can be an effective means of reducing pollution
  and saving taxpayers money by lowering wastewater treatment
  costs. Michigan, New York and other states have limited
  phosphate levels in detergents.

° States should encourage stricter enforcement of water protection laws. Charging polluters and giving citizens an
  incentive to help enforce the law would stretch resources.

<u>FOR FURTHER INFORMATION</u>

<u>Publications</u>

<u>Building a Water Quality Consensus: Key Issues for the 80's</u>.
Available from Margaret Downs at the Northeast-Midwest Institute, 530 House Annex #2, Washington, D.C. 20515 (202) 225-1082.

<u>Participation in the Construction Grants Program: Accoun-
ting, Auditing, and Financial Considerations</u>. A practical
set of handbooks about sewage treatment. Available from
Harvey Coldman at Arthur Young & Company, 227 Park Avenue,
New York, NY, 10177 (212) 922-2100.

<u>Friday Morning Letter</u>. The monthly newsletter of the
American Clean Water Association which describes problems,
solutions and trends in the field of water and waste management.

<u>America In Ruins: Beyond the Public Works Pork Barrel</u>, by
Pat Choate and Susan Walter, 1981, Council of State Planning
Agencies. A comprehensive survey of the nation warns that
deteriorating public facilities threaten national economic ruin
unless new ways are found to finance public works. Available
for $9.95 from the Conference on Alternative State and Local
Policies, 2000 Florida Avenue, N.W., Washington, D.C. 20009

<u>Organizations</u>

ENVIRONMENTAL POLICY INSTITUTE, 317 Pennsylvania Ave., S.E.,
Washington, D.C., 20003 (202) 547-5330. Research on water
conservation and analyses of state water conservation laws.
Contact Brent Blackwelder.

NATIONAL DEMONSTRATION WATER PROJECT, Edwin Cobb, Director,
1725 De Sales Street, N.W., Washington, D.C., 20036 (202) 659-
0661. NDWP and its affiliates around the country give practical
assistance to communities in solving water and waste problems
and train sewage workers.

AMERICAN CLEAN WATER ASSOCIATION, Larry Silverman, Executive
Director, 1341 G Street, N.W., Washington, D.C., 20005 (202) 638-
3014. A professional association providing technical assistance
to communities on wastewater problems.

CLEAN WATER ACTION PROJECT, David Zwick, Executive Director,
1341 G Street, N.W., Suite 204, Washington, D.C., 20005 (202)
638-1196. Public interest consumer lobby working on a wide
range of clean water and drinking water issues. CLEAN WATER FUND,
same address, (202) 638-3013, works with state and local
officials to help communities develop creative and workable
ways to finance their water and infrastructure needs.

Prepared by David Zwick and Ed Hopkins

Labor and Work

Labor Legislation

BACKGROUND FACTS

In July 1982, 9.8% of Americans were out of work, according to the Bureau of Labor Statistics.

Among blacks and hispanics, however, the rate was even higher -- 18.5% and 13.9%, respectively.

One out of every five Americans will experience unemployment in some form in this year. Unemployment compensation checks will cover only some of the unemployment, and only part of the wages lost through unemployment.

Having a job in America doesn't necessarily mean you aren't poor. Eighty percent of the heads of poor households work, but only one-third of them full-time and year round. For poor people who can work, then, the problem is not just being able to find a job, but being able to find a stable job or a well-paying one.

As a national average, 20.8% of non-agriculture related workers belong to a union. New York has the largest percentage of its labor force belonging to a union (39.2%); North Carolina the lowest (6.5%). A major reason for this low number is the "right-to-work" laws in twenty states which present a major obstacle to union organizing.

Working conditions are often poor and workers are injured or get sick as a result. Many jobs expose workers to the risk of crippling or fatal accidents or potentially fatal diseases. Conservative government estimates suggest that between 115,000 and 200,000 Americans die each year from an occupationally-related accident or disease.

Many workers also face serious employment-related problems because they have relatively little control over their working conditions. Problems can sometimes flow from this common source. The less influence workers have over the pace and organization of work, the more vulnerable they may be to health and safety problems. The less protection workers have against arbitrary dismissal and supervisory abuse, the more difficulties they may have with sudden layoffs and intermittent employment.

<u>THE PROBLEM</u>

Unemployment, low wages, occupational injuries and diseases, and powerful and arbitrary employers are too often the facts of life for America's workers.

Over the last 50 years, the labor movement and liberal organizations have passed precedent-setting national legislation to help and assist workers in all facets of their life, including the National Labor Relations Act, the Davis-Bacon Act, Occupational Safety and Health Act, and unemployment compensation, workmen's compensation, and minimum wage laws. These federal laws certainly need to be broadened and strengthened.

However, at this time an administration is in power in Washington which is committed to weakening all of these protections. It is imperative, therefore, that state governments accept increased responsibility for protecting working people.

Unemployment insurance is a worker's first line of defense against the hardships of unemployment. Benefits are due workers who have enough qualifying wages and yearly work experience to meet their state's minimum conditions, who are free from disqualification on the basis of their separation from their last place of employment, and who are ready, willing, and able to work.

Although based on federal law, unemployment compensation is administered by the states; and states, controlling many of its most critical features, have in some cases modified the program to improve worker conditions. Victims of lockouts are able to collect benefits in sixteen states. The definition of "suitable work" includes fringe benefits in the states of Indiana and Michigan. Twelve states have no waiting period before benefits begin. And in California, a short-time compensation program exists which mitigates the impact of layoffs by allowing employees to retain workers during temporary slowdowns and pay them partial unemployment insurance benefits.

Maximum state unemployment compensation does not replace a worker's total salary, and the minimum weekly amounts are often far below the poverty level. In addition, the complex set of requirements often exclude many from receiving benefits at all, while the maximum number of weeks during which a worker can receive benefits is often limited. The unemployment compensation that the average unemployed person "enjoys" is not the equivalent of a paid vacation, but a massive slash in his or her standard of living.

Many workers have little control over the pace and
organization of work, health and safety conditions, wage
determination, and job security. Likewise, employees who
wish to "blow the whistle" on illegal consumer or environmental
activity by their employer have few powers to resist employer
attempts at intimidation, discrimination, or retribution for
disclosing information. Unionization and collective bargaining,
and applying the concept of an employee "bill of rights" to
the workplace are two ways to address these problems and
increase the "say" that workers have at their jobs.

In other areas, state legislatures passed a number of
interesting pieces of union oriented legislation, even in the
conservative years of 1980 and 1981. Michigan, Ohio, and
Wisconsin prohibited the awarding of state contracts to
persons or firms found to be in violation of the National
Labor Relations Act. California joined this group of states
in 1981, and passed a similar measure. In five states --
Connecticut, Illinois, Louisiana, Ohio, and Oregon -- individual statutes were amended to protect a worker who reports a
violation of law or participates in an enforcement proceeding.

Some states are improving their labor programs. Washington and Ohio have upgraded benefits for their citizens by
eliminating private insurance carriers from their compensation
program and substituting an exclusive state fund instead.
Through Washington's exclusive state fund, eligible workers
receive $1.05 in benefits for every dollar paid in premiums
thanks to the program's investment earnings, which more than
offset the entire expense of administering the program.
Washington's approach contrasts sharply with states in which
private insurers pocket $.48 of every premium dollar, leaving
ill and injured workers only $.52 per dollar. With the help
of state AFL-CIO's, legislators in New York, Rhode Island,
Michigan, and Illinois are working on similar bills to create
exclusive state funds.

Ohio's program has wide public support, as shown in the
last election in which voters rejected by a 4 to 1 margin an
insurance industry-sponsored initiative that would have
allowed private insurance companies to compete with the state
program to sell worker's compensation insurance.

Progressives, concerned about the weakening of OSHA and
the Reagan-inspired attack on worker health and safety, are
also seeking to pass tough right-to-know laws, which would
allow employees to know about the hazardous chemicals they work
with. Excellent legislation has already been passed in the
cities of Philadelphia and Cincinnati and in the states of
California, Connecticut, Maine, Michigan, New York and West
Virginia.

<u>WHAT STATES CAN DO</u>

<u>Reforming Unemployment Insurance</u>

° States should increase benefit levels to a higher percent
  of the claimant's average weekly wage.

° States should increase the number of weeks of compensation
  coverage. Most states have pegged this level at 26 weeks.

° States should lift "waiting week restrictions" to allow
  claimants to recieve their benefits immediately and eliminate
  specific "actively seeking work" availability requirements
  and instead require job search efforts that are appropriate.

° States should enact laws which allow victims of employer
  lockouts to collect benefits, and allow unemployment benefits
  to be paid to strikers after a seven week waiting period.

° States should protect the jobless' right to obtain benefits.
  Employers should be required to post notices of unemployment
  insurance rights in prominent places and hearings should be
  held prior to a cut-off of benefits.

<u>Protecting and Expanding Workers' Rights</u>

° States with "right-to-work" laws should repeal them.

° States should prohibit the awarding of state contracts to
  persons or firms found to be in violation of the National
  Labor Relations Act.

° States should pass a "whistleblowers" protection act which
  prohibits reprisals against a public or private sector
  employee who reports any violation of state, local or
  federal law, or who participates in an investigation,
  hearing, inquiry or court action.

<u>Establishing Decent Wages</u>

° States should enact or continue "little Davis-Bacon" acts
  which set prevailing wage standards for construction work
  financed by state monies.

° States should pass laws to provide for tougher enforcement
  of state minimum wages.

<u>Increasing Worker Health and Safety</u>

° States should reform their workman's compensation system to
  include broader eligibility, improved benefits, and greater
  availability of medical care to meet with the standards suggested
  by the National Commission on State Workmen's Compensation Laws.

<u>FOR FURTHER INFORMATION</u>

<u>Publications</u>

     <u>AFL-CIO Federationist</u>, AFL-CIO. A monthly magazine
which publishes excellent articles on unemployment compensation, workman's compensation, and other labor issues.

     <u>Short Time Compensation and Work Sharing: A New Alter-
native to Layoffs</u>, 1980, Fred Best and James Mattessich.
Washington D.C. Council of State Planning Agencies.

     <u>State Workers' Compensation Laws</u>, 1981, US Department of
Labor, Employment Standards Division. Reviews state laws.

     <u>The Working Poor</u>, David Gordon, 1980, Washington, D.C.
Council of State Planning Agencies. Shows what can be done
by a state to expand the economy's share of "good jobs."

     <u>The New Right: A Growing Force in State Politics</u>,
Will Hunter, 1980. Washington, D.C., Conference on State and
Local Policies. Comprehensive report on "New Right" activities
including right-to-work efforts and attacks on prevailing wage

     <u>Towards Full Employment: New Directions for State and
Local Government</u>, 1982. Washington, D.C., Conference on Alternative State and Local Policies. A comprehensive look at
what state and local governments can do to increase employment.

<u>Organizations</u>

AFL-CIO, 815 16th St., N.W., Washington, D.C., 20006 (202)
637-5000. Membership organization of private and public
sector trade unions, researching national, state, and local
labor legislation programs.

CONFERENCE ON ALTERNATIVE STATE AND LOCAL POLICIES, 2000
Florida Ave., N.W., Washington, D.C., 20009 (202) 387-6030.
Lee Webb, Executive Director. Publishes studies on employment
and labor programs and periodic updates on new state legislation.

CITIZEN ACTION, 1501 Euclid Ave., Suite 500, Cleveland, OH,
44115 (216) 861-5200. Umbrella organization of nine statewide
citizen action groups. Working on range of employment-related
issues, ilncluding right-to-know legislation and workers compensation.

Prepared by William Schweke.

Public Employees

<u>BACKGROUND FACTS</u>

Thirteen million people work for state and local government. Until recently, state and local government was the fastest growing sector of our economy, accounting for 16 per cent of the U.S. workforce.

Roughly half of all state and local government employees are represented by a union. However, many public workers do not have true collective bargaining rights. The basic protections gained by private sector workers and the National Labor Relations Act 47 years ago are still denied to many public employees.

The number of public employees has been decreasing since 1980, yet few jurisdictions have addressed job security issues such as retraining, recall rights, severance pay, and voluntary early retirement.

The growth of technology is also changing working conditions for thousands of public employees. For example, the use of video display terminals speeds up work and creates new health hazards; mechanized refuse collection sometimes results in smaller crews and reduced service; and computerization of information services threatens to downgrade the pay and training requirements for librarians.

Although public employees are specifically excluded from Occupational Safety and Health Act coverage (which protects all private sector workers), they are exposed to a wide variety of hazards. In fact, National Safety Council statistics show that government workers are generally injured over two-and-one-half times as often as private industry workers, and those injuries are over twice as severe.

Women traditionally have been segregated into a small number of occupations in the workforce. Since these jobs have been undervalued, there is a substantial earnings gap between male and female wages. The average woman now earns 59¢ for every $1.00 the average man earns. These disparities have been documented in many public jurisdictions.

As public jurisdictions face reduced revenues from the recession and federal budget cuts, there is an increased effort to contract out public services to private profit-making firms. Contracting out is seen as the answer to high costs and inefficiency, yet often is an excuse for justifying poor management.

<u>THE PROBLEM</u>

Public employees confront four major issues in their work: collective bargaining, elimination of jobs, workplace safety and health, and contracting out of work.

Public workers have attained union recognition and the right to collective bargaining in a variety of ways on a state-by-state, city-by-city basis. There are roughly 80,000 local governments in the U.S., 40,000 multi-purpose and 40,000 single-purpose -- aside from the 50 states. Each of these independent jurisdictions has its own wage system, classification plan, and benefit levels.

In some jurisdictions bargaining came about through law, the first such public sector bargaining law being enacted 23 years ago for local government employees in Wisconsin. In other jurisdictions, bargaining has come about by way of Executive Order. And in many states, bargaining rights were achieved on a "de facto" basis with local governments throughout the state.

This absurd system of public sector labor relations is grossly unfair to state and local government employees. Most bargaining laws have at least some inequitable features not contained in the law governing private sector relationships. No two state laws are the same; in fact, many states have more than one law covering public workers.

The 1976 U.S. Supreme Court decision in <u>National League of Cities</u> vs. <u>Usery</u> chilled the prospects for enactment of federal legislation to establish a rational framework for labor relations in state and local governments. Since this decision, only three states have enacted new collective bargaining legislation for uncovered employees.

The most common argument for denying public employees bargaining rights and the right to strike is that public employees have an adequate alternative to the bargaining process in the various civil service statutes and other ordinances that protect their rights. Yet most aspects of civil service systems are actually the personnel arm of the government -- akin to personnel departments in private enterprises.

Public employees have been decreasing in numbers since 1980. Some of the loss in public employment results from shifts in service delivery from the public to the private sector. Still greater portions of the job loss stem from the federal government's cutbacks in assistance to state and local governments, and from the effects of recession and inflation.

The decline in public sector employment threatens the mission of government: to assist and protect the disadvantaged and to provide those goods and services which the private sector is unable or unwilling to supply. For example, workers in institutional and community mental health facilities throughout the country are faced with threats of closures, phase-downs, budget cuts, and contracting out. Thousands of workers have already been laid off.

Although new technology has the potential to offer safer working conditions, the opportunity to perform more skilled work and more efficient delivery of services, this potential often is not realized. Experience shows that new technology may make jobs more routine, more unskilled, more unhealthy, lower-paying and more dead-end.

Public employees are not automatically covered by the federal Occupational Safety and Health Act (OSHA) and less than half of the states provide safety and health protections for public employees. When a state does have some coverage, it is often less stringent than that of OSHA. Even where OSHA coverage is available, there is less protection because the Reagan administration is seeking to weaken its provisions.

The historic segregation of women workers in a small number of traditionally female occupations has resulted in substantial disparities between male and female wages. This is certainly true in public employment. This earnings gap is rooted in discrimination, since society systematically undervalues work performed by women. "Women's jobs" pay less than "men's jobs" involving comparable skill, effort and responsibility. Pay equity for all workers cannot be achieved as long as employers deny equitable pay to workers in female-dominated job classifications.

The drive to contract out public services to private, profit-making firms continues at an increasing pace in many jurisdictions throughout the country. With state and local governments facing reduced revenues from the recession and federal budget cuts, many public officials mistakenly view contracting out as the cure-all. While government managers can sometimes achieve short-term solutions which slash personnel costs, they do not consider long-term budgetary and service considerations. In addition, public officials too often exaggerate the value of contracting out as the answer to high costs and inefficiency.

The private delivery of public services has, in many cases, resulted in higher costs, poorer services, decreased accountability and corruption. The Urban Institute, a private, nonprofit research organization, concluded in its 1978 study that the long-term benefits were "uncertain."

<u>WHAT STATES CAN DO</u>

<u>Collective Bargaining</u>

° States should give public sector workers full rights and
  protections to organize and bargain collectively in individual states and jurisdictions within the states.

<u>Jobs</u>

° States should negotiate improved job protections and provide
  alternatives to layoffs, such as the rearrangment of budget
  priorities and alternative revenue sources; retraining;
  transfer rights; severance pay; moving expenses; the use of
  attrition instead of layoffs; and voluntary early retirement.

° State should establish career development programs which
  provide equitable opportunities for public workers to
  obtain promotions.

° States should use trial periods and advance notification
  to allow time for careful implementation when new technology
  is introduced.

° States should support the use of technologies designed to
  improve and expand public services.

<u>Safety and Health at Work</u>

° States should enact laws establishing safety and health plans
  covering public employees that incorporate, at a minimum,
  federal OSHA standards. States should establish their own
  OSHA plans, using Connecticut as an example.

° States should ensure that public employees are provided a
  safe and healthy place of work free from recognized or
  suspected hazards. The right of employees to refuse unsafe
  work should be recognized.

<u>Pay Equity</u>

° States should commit themselves to pay equity and, working
  through contract negotiations and administrative actions,
  upgrade undervalued job classifications. All job evaluation
  studies should investigate the pay equity issue.

<u>Contracting Out</u>

° States should consider the real costs and disadvantages of
  proposals to contract out any public work traditionally
  performed by public employees, including possible higher
  costs, reduced or poorer service, lack of public control,
  and possible corruption.

FOR FURTHER INFORMATION

Publications

     Summary of Public Sector Labor Relations Policies, U.S.
Department of Labor, Labor-Management Services Administration,
1981. Reviews status of laws in each state with respect to
bargaining rights, strike policy, etc.

     Labor-Management Relations in State and Local Governments,
Bureau of the Census, Special Studies No. 102, November 1981.
Analyzes state and local government agreements: the number of
agreements between government and unions, and the kinds of
governments concerned.

     Pay Equity: A Union Issue for the 1980's. American Federa-
tion of State, County and Municipal Employees, 1980.

     Occupational Health and Safety of Municipal Workers,
Urban Environment Conference, August 1977. Proceedings of a
series of regional conferences outlining issues on occupational
health and safety of municipal workers.

     Government for $ale, John Hanrahan. American Federation
of State, County and Municipal Employees, 1977. Details
problems of contracting out government work to the private
sector, especially problems of possible corruption and abuse.

     Manual on Pay Equity: Raising Wages for Women's Work.
Conference on Alternative State and Local Policies, 1980, $9.95.
Comprehensive manual of facts and figures, detailed analysis of
federal, state and local laws, and strategies for organizing.

Organizations

AMERICAN FEDERATION OF STATE, COUNTY AND MUNICIPAL EMPLOYEES,
1625 L St., N.W., Washington, D.C., 20036 (202) 452-4800.
Linda Lampkin, Director, Department of Research. Excellent
source of information on policies affecting public employees.
Does lobbying and provides political support.

PUBLIC EMPLOYEE DEPARTMENT, AFL-CIO, 815 16th St., N.W.,
Washington, D.C., 20006 (202) 393-2820. Provides updates on
issues affecting public employees.

NATIONAL EDUCATION ASSOCIATION, 1201 16th St., N.W., Washington,
D.C., 20036 (202) 822-7300. Largest organization of teachers.
Provides information on wages, salaries, and issues affecting
public education.

Prepared by Linda Lampkin.

Workplace Safety and Health

<u>BACKGROUND FACTS</u>

Death and disease in the workplace is an omnipresent fact of life for millions of American workers. Scientific research conducted in the 1970s leads to one conclusion: the magnitude of the occupational injury and disease problem is greater than the framers of the Occupational Safety and Health act in the 1960s ever expected.

Problems such as excessive exposure to lead, cotton dust, mercury and silica have not disappeared, and new issues keep surfacing -- for example, discovery of brain tumors in petrochemical industry workers.

Reasonable estimates of job-related cancer suggest that as many as 40,000-50,000 workers will die in 1982. All these cancers could have been prevented if exposure to workplace carcinogens had not occurred. Moreover, there is reason to believe that the human toll may grow worse in the decades ahead. Because the average latency for human cancer is twenty years or more, it is likely that current cancer deaths are a reflection of past exposures during early expansion of the petrochemical industry. Impairment of workers' children from parental chemical exposure may represent a problem as severe as occupational cancer. Thus, the precautions taken in the next few years will determine whether occupational cancer will rise in the 21st century.

Cancer, reproductive impairment, chronic lung disease and neurologic toxicity all have emerged as major occupational health problems. In addition, concern has grown about new health hazards, such as indoor air pollution, job-related stress, health effects of new energy technology, radiation (both ionizing and non-ionizing), hazards of machine-paced work, and continuous work on visual display terminals.

The passage of the Occupational Safety and Health Act (OSHA) of 1970 was heralded as landmark legislation which assured for every worker the right to a safe and healthful workplace. One often-stated argument for the enactment of federal legislation was the dismal performance of state occupational safety and health programs in protecting the lives of workers. As a result, the federal government was given a major role in the new legislation; states were allowed to run their own programs only if they were proven to be "at least as effective" as the federal OSHA efforts.

<u>THE PROBLEM</u>

Ironically, twelve years after the enactment of OSHA, states need to play an increasing role in protecting the gains of the 1970s and in expanding worker protections beyond that which currently exists. Yet state OSHA program performance was at best mixed during the Carter administration, though some states -- for example, California, Michigan and Minnesota -- have been at least equal to the federal effort, and in many respects, stronger.

Under Reagan, OSHA is undergoing planned disassembly and decline. Enforcement, training and education, standard setting, protection of worker rights to participate, funding, staffing and research, have all been hit. For example, the number of inspectors has declined by 29%; monthly inspections by 17%; follow-up inspections by 68% and serious citations by 27%. Some regulations have been withdrawn; others are not being enforced.

With the Reagan administration's focus on deregulation rather than protecting workers' health, the need to improve state programs once again has become paramount.

In general, state record-keeping systems are not designed to facilitate recognition of work-related problems. Improved data collection systems are mandatory if effective research is to be carried out to identify and assess work-related disease. California has recently passed legislation which establishes a Birth Defects Registry designed to quantify increased risk to reproduction from toxic substance exposure. Connecticut operates a Tumor Registry and Los Angeles County has a tumor registry with promising experience in identifying high risk populations. States should consider establishing both tumor and birth defects/spontaneous abortion registries.

The acid test for workers' rights is whether workers have the right to know the identity and the hazards of sub- stances they work with. Right-to-know legislation has been passed in nine states and several localities. Most of these laws have basically the same purpose: to ensure that workers know the hazards of substances they work with and that the government and local citizens know where toxic materials are used or handled.

State and local toxics laws are most useful if they are enacted to protect both workers and the public. Casting state and local laws with a broad scope that includes protecting the public health and adequately preparing for local emergency services will also protect such laws from the federal preemption threatened by the Reagan administration.

Right-to-know legislation provides for access to information but does not require duty to warn. Duty to warn law would represent a significant improvement over the current important but limited right-to-know statutes. Employers should have a clear duty to inform workers when they are exposed to hazardous substances or conditions rather than simply make information available. Such legislation should include both civil and criminal penalties to be most effective.

Additional remedial legislation needs to be considered at the state level to expand worker rights beyond those already guaranteed by OSHA, including:

° Increasing the maximum penalties for willful, failure to abate repeated, and serious violations of the OSH Act.

° Expanding workers' right-to-refuse hazardous work. Workers who face life-threatening hazards including exposure to carcinogens (the effect of which may not be manifested until ten to twenty years later) should have the right-of-refusal to work where an imminent hazard exists. When they refuse to work because of an imminent danger, their pay should not be docked.

° Adding provisions on rate retention and "walk around" pay. In order to encourage workers to participate in a medical surveillance program, they cannot be penalized (such as by loss of wages). Rate retention is a unique and crucial provision to facilitate participation in health-monitoring programs.

  Walk around pay is based on similar considerations. Legislation which guarantees an employee representative pay during an inspection by an OSHA compliance officer will augment the right to participate in a OSHA walk around.

° Safety and health legislation designed to increase workers' rights and participation would expand the private right of action of workers. Safety and health legislation should not limit rights of workers to such relief through the courts. Enabling legislation will be required in most states to ensure citizens' rights of redress.

° Revenue for state safety and health programs could be generated through worker's compensation programs in which insurance premiums from industry designed to fund various programs would be based upon the size of a particular payroll and the actuarial status of the company. The state of Washington is a prime example of the use of funds from worker's compensation to support research and education programs.

WHAT STATES CAN DO

State OSHA Programs

° States with OSHA programs should consider increasing maximum
  penalties for willful failure to abate and repeated citations.

° States should adopt legislation guaranteeing walk-around
  pay and rate retention during temporary medical removal
  protection.

Right to Know Legislation

° States should pass worker right-to-know legislation to
  ensure that 1) workers know the identity and the hazards
  of the substances with which they work, and 2) that the
  public is informed to toxic chemicals being used.

° States should pass legislation which supplements right-to-
  know legislation with an affirmative duty to warn, and gives
  workers the right to refuse to perform unsafe work.

State Centers

° States should establish Centers for Occupational Safety
  and Health Research, Service and Training. California has
  adopted legislation which established two state-funded
  occupational health centers to upgrade and expand the
  resources of the state in the area of occupational health
  and medicine.

Legal Rights

° States should enact legislation which provides for private
  right of action by workers in order that they sue to correct
  hazards rather than being wholly dependent on departments
  of labor or health.

Record Keeping

° States should adopt legislation to establish birth defects,
  spontaneous abortion and cancer registries which are coded
  for industry and occupation. In addition, they should
  ensure that death certificates are coded for industry and
  occupation to facilitate identification of work-related
  mortality.

Reproductive Rights

° States should enact legislation creating or strengthening
  laws applicable to the use of carcinogens and to chemicals
  which cause reproductive impairment.

<u>FOR FURTHER INFORMATION</u>

<u>Publications</u>

Kaminski, R. et al., <u>American Journal of Public Health</u>, 71, 525-526, 1981. Discussion of coding death certificates.

<u>Reproductive Hazards in the Workplace - A Resource Guide</u>, Coalition for The Reproductive Rights of Workers 1971 I Street, N.W., Washington, D.C., 20006. A resource guide to issues of reproductive impairment from chemical and physical agents in the workplace.

Davis, D. et al., in <u>Banbury Report 9 - Quantification of Occupational Cancer</u>, Edited by Richard Peto and Marvin Schneiderman, Cold Spring Harbor Laboratory, 1981. A thorough discussion of the problems in estimating cancer causes. The entire report is a useful source book on occupational cancer.

Ashford, Nicholas, <u>Crisis in the Workplace: Occupational Disease and Injury</u>, MIT Press: Cambridge, Mass., 1976. Describes the role of state programs prior to enactment of OSHA, and generally is a useful source book on occupational safety and health.

<u>Labor Studies Journal</u>, 6(1), Spring 1981. Edited by Steven Oeutsch. The entire journal is devoted to the theme of occupational safety and health. The final three articles are devoted to resources. Available from Transaction Periodicals Consortium, Box L, Rutgers University, New Brunswick, NJ, 08903.

<u>Organizations</u>

AFL-CIO DEPARTMENT OF OCCUPATIONAL SAFETY AND HEALTH, Room 507, 815 16th Street, N.W., Washington, D.C., 20006 (202) 637-5174 or 5366. Extensive material on right-to-know laws and the Reagan Administration's policies on occupational safety and health.

COALITION FOR THE REPRODUCTIVE RIGHTS OF WORKERS, 1917 I Street, N.W., Suite 201, Washington, D.C., 20006.

OCCUPATIONAL CANCER CONTROL UNIT, 2151 Berkeley Way, Berkeley, CA 94704, (415) 843-7900. Information on California's cancer control legislation.

HAZARD EVALUATION SYSTEM AND INFORMATION SERVICE (THESIS), 2151 Berkeley Way, Room 504, Berkeley, CA, 94704 (415) 540-2012. Cancer and reproductive impairment information, including information on the California Birth Defects Registry.

Prepared by John Froines.

Civil & Human Rights

Citizens with Disabilities

BACKGROUND FACTS

There are an estimated 36 to 45 million persons with disabilities in the United States. Every community has a significant number of disabled persons with a variety of needs.

Substantial numbers of disabled people are prevented from becoming active participants in their community by the following barriers: architectural design, lack of ability to communicate with others, insecurity of basic survival needs, lack of transportation, exclusion and other forms of discrimination, lack of community-based services, and inadequate education.

Research shows that for every dollar spent on rehabilitation and training programs for disabled persons, six dollars is recaptured in tax revenues when the disabled person begins work. Yet current cuts in social programs will reduce the number of disabled people who can receive this training. Similarly, the future of independent living programs, aimed at enhancing the self-sufficiency of disabled people, is in doubt.

Recent decisions by the Reagan Administration pertaining to auto safety, occupational health and safety, and environmental protection will result in increased numbers of disabled persons, either from birth defects, accident or exposure to toxic chemicals. Yet as resources for human services become scarce, it is likely that disabled people will lose the services and benefits designed to make them more independent and able to tend to their own needs.

While federal legislation mandates that disabled children receive a free and appropriate public education with services and equipment to meet their needs, the federal government has never provided the full funding required by the law to insure disabled children of their rights.

For people with severe and multiple handicaps, it is cheaper and more effective to provide community-based services in home-like settings than to confine them, warehouse fashion, in large, isolated institutions. Yet, even though a small percentage of all severely disabled people reside in large institutions, the bulk of money spent by the federal government for such persons goes to institutions.

Civil rights laws and regulations which provide access to education, housing, transportation, employment and other esssentials have been targeting by the Reagan administration for "regulatory reform" or dismantling.

<u>THE PROBLEM</u>

The 1970s marked the beginning of innovative legislation and programs recognizing that an individual's potential was not predetermined by severity or type of disability.

The appropriate government response to the problems of disabled, then, is to promote the potential of each person. New approaches include: prohibiting discrimination against qualified disabled persons at the federal and state levels; expanding the coverage of rehabilitation programs to insure severely disabled people are trained for jobs; eliminating disincentives in benefit programs which prevent disabled people from seeking jobs; assuring that federally-funded buildings, including federal housing, are accessible to and usable by disabled people and creation of independent living programs, operated by disabled people at the local level, to provide advocacy and services. Disabled people could live as independently as possible in their own communities, rather than in nursing homes and institutions.

The Reagan Administration has accelerated the review process for Supplemental Security Income (SSI) and Supplemental Security for the Disabled Income (SSDI) claimants in an effort to drastically reduce the number of beneficiaries. Thousands of disabled persons have lost their only source of income without a face-to-face examination by the reviewers. Of those who have appealed their terminations, a vast majority have won because they are not able to work. However, many do not appeal. And even those who win their appeals must wait for months, living on nothing, before their cases are heard.

As the role of the federal government in relation to the states and local governments is changing, and as budget cuts are endangering the existence of community services, the gains of disabled persons in the U.S. are in jeopardy.

The rationale behind recent policy innovation is that disabled people have a right, as citizens of this country, to expect a minimum level of support and civil rights protection from the government. This ideological approach rejects past notions that disabled people are best served by charities and welfare programs (which do not envision the disabled person as a valuable community member with potential for leadership and self-sufficiency.) It also rejects the medical approach to resolving the disability problems, in which disabled people are viewed as sick or deviant and must be cured or taken care of.

Implementation of these new programs and civil rights protections have met with two principal arguments: 1) that the cost of providing services to and making accommodations for disabled people is too high, and 2) that there aren't that

many disabled people who want to actively participate in
their communities, travel or work.

The cost argument ignores the enormous costs currently
being paid for programs that do little or nothing to increase
the self-sufficiency and skills of disabled people. These
include: state hospitals for people with mental retardation
and other disabilities in which, historically, abuses and
regression have been the rule; benefit programs like Supplemental Security Income, which keep people dependent on benefits
for the rest of their lives, rather than actively seeking
training and eventual employment; medical benefit programs
which do not pay for independent living training and equipment
and which instead force people into expensive hospital settings
for medical care; expensive, separate special schools for
disabled children to which they must be bused, at additional
cost; separate transportation services which require additional
drivers, vehicles, fuel and other costs. These and other
expensive programs are designed to keep disabled people
outside of the mainstream of community life.

It is impossible to ignore the fact that there are
millions of disabled people in this country, and that there
are expenses involved in responding to their existence.
State and local policy makers must decide whether that response
is planned to increase their ability to participate in the
community, and to pay for those expenses in taxes, or to
further segregate, isolate and ensure that they will never
be able to contribute.

In the coming decades, as the numbers of disabled people
increase, this issue will become more crucial. The issue,
then, is how money is spent, rather than how much.

The second argument -- that disabled people don't really
want to take advantage of opportunities to participate actively
-- ignores the growing movement of disabled people who are
organizing at the grass roots level. There are dozens of
disabled people's organizations in most states, and they have
changed from the social clubs of the past into politically
active and sophisticated groups. Increasing numbers of
disabled people have enrolled at colleges and universities
in pursuit of skills and degrees that will yield jobs. As
disabled people receive an education, their expectations
rise. This leads to growing numbers of disabled persons who
can take advantage of increased accessibility and opportunities.

<u>WHAT STATES CAN DO</u>

Civil Rights

° States should pass legislation prohibiting discrimination
  on the basis of disability. States must recognize that
  discrimination against disabled people poses a substantial
  barrier to their independence. Many employers, for instance,
  use old and arbitrary hiring policies which screen out
  qualified disabled job applicants. Unless disabled
  people can take advantage of state laws prohibiting such
  discrimination, they cannot become independent taxpayers.

Education

° States should pass legislation ensuring the educational
  rights of disabled children. State legislation should contain the same rights, procedures and safeguards as the
  federal Education for All Handicapped Children Act. As
  the federal government reduces its role in this area,
  states must ensure that disabled children receive a free
  and appropriate education.

Independent Living

° States should enact legislation creating independent living
  programs. These programs, with relatively small budgets,
  provide crucial services which keep disabled persons out of
  residential or medical facilities costing much more than
  community living arrangements.

° States should restructure their in-home support services to
  allow disabled people to hire, fire and supervise their own
  attendants, who provide homemaker, chore-type services.
  Such a program has been in effect in California for nearly a
  decade. It allows people with very severe disabilities to
  remain in the community and avoids the exorbitant costs of
  institutionalization. Because the disabled person is in
  direct control of the attendant, there is no bureaucratic
  structure to take away flexibility to arrange for one's own
  needs. This also gives the disabled person supervisory
  experience. The costs of implementing such a system are
  less than using private companies which often charge high
  administrative fees.

<u>FOR FURTHER INFORMATION</u>

<u>Publications</u>

<u>The Legal Rights of Handicapped Persons</u>, Robert L. Bergdorf, Paul H. Brookes Publishing Co., 1980.

<u>The Unexpected Minority</u>, John Glideman and William Roth, Harcourt Brace Javanovich, 1980.

<u>Handicapping America: Barriers to People</u>, Frank Bowe, Harper and Row, 1978.

"Independent Living: From Social Movement to Analytic Paradigm," Gerben DeJong, <u>Archives of Physical Medicine and Rehabilitation</u>, October 1979.

<u>Organizations</u>

DISABILITY RIGHTS EDUCATION AND DEFENSE FUND, INC., 2032 San Pablo Ave., Berkeley, CA, 94702. Robert Funk, Director/Attorney. A legal rights and public policy organization focusing on the civil rights of disabled persons.

DISABILITY RIGHTS CENTER, 1346 Connecticut Ave., N.W., Washington, D.C. 20036, Evan Kemp, Director. A legal rights group focusing on consumer rights for medical devices and federal affirmative action laws for disabled workers.

CHILDREN'S DEFENSE FUND, 1520 New Hampshire Ave., N.W., Washington, D.C. 20036. Legal rights organization with an excellent component specializing in the rights of disabled children, especially in education.

ASSOCIATION FOR RETARDED CITIZENS, 1522 K St., N.W., Washington, D.C. 20005. An association with chapters in the states; a strong advocate for the rights of persons with mental retardation and services for them. Their governmental affairs office has information about legislation at the state and federal level.

UNITED CEREBRAL PALSY ASSOCIATIONS, INC., 2021 K St., N.W., Washington, D.C. 20006. Information and programs about state and local policies that provide for maximum self-sufficiency for persons with severe disabilities.

Prepared by Debbie Kaplan.

Civil Rights

<u>BACKGROUND FACTS</u>

Civil rights issues in American society are at a critical point.

In the 1960's and early 1970's this nation's commitment to equality of opportunity and to prevention of discrimination based on race, sex, age, religion, national origin, or disabil- ity was translated into a series of laws designed to transform this commitment into a reality backed by federal enforcement.

This commitment remained firm in the 1970s. Congress, under the leadership of Presidents Nixon, Ford, and Carter, passed further legislation to fill gaps in the basic laws and to strengthen the enforcement powers of the federal government. Those federal agencies charged with enforcing civil rights laws actively pursued abuses, and substantial resources were allocated them to that end.

These gains are rapidly being eroded under a tide of conservatism, apathy and a loss of confidence in the American political system.

In all three areas of major civil rights legislation -- voting, housing and employment -- legislative protections are being "evaluated". For months, the existence of the Voting Rights Act of 1965 hung precariously in the balance on Capitol Hill; tougher anti-discriminatory housing legislation has been forestalled; and the backbone of societal equality -- employment discrimination legislation -- is facing attack from both the administration and a seemingly less vigilant Supreme Court.

Equality in the workplace has not become a reality. 66,569 charges of discrimination were filed nationwide in fiscal year 1979-1980, according to EEOC.

The unemployment rates of minorities remains at twice the level of whites, and women in the labor market earned only 60% the income of their male counterparts.

Over two-thirds of our disabled citizens were unemployed or underemployed.

Recent Supreme Court decisions such as <u>Texas Department of Community Affairs v. Joyce Ann Burdine</u>, have shifted the burden of proof of discrimination to the aggrieved party.

Action is necessary in the face of losses of legislated civil rights protections. Litigation is one alternative, but for most the cost is prohibitive. The more logical and far reaching alternative is to put the bite back into existent civil rights legislation, and to establish watchdog groups to ensure that civil rights legislation and its enforcement are constant protections.

In times of economic recession, those groups historically out of the mainstream of economic and social equality are affected to a greater degree than more affluent groups. Thus unemployment rates for Blacks, Hispanics, and Mexican Americans which have always been higher than those for White Americans, continue to increase and while women have achieved a measure of advancement in the workplace, the defeat of ERA serves notice that in this area also, white males will continue to dominate.

Economic hardship seems to lessen concern about societal equality and deepen interest in individual gain. While white middle class America is struggling to maintain its standard of living, voting rights, equitable housing, and adequate schooling are lofty goals for which minorities must now fight alone. No longer do the widespread coalitions of the 1960s and 1970s exist which fought for solutions for societal ills. College campuses, once the centers for organized protest and change, have turned to directing students into the mainstream and teaching them saleable skills for the job market. In short, apathy and lack of organization have infected the civil rights struggle of the 1980s.

Anti-civil rights sentiment has been manifested recently in the attitude of those on Capitol Hill. Many Reagan administration officials exhibit lukewarm attitudes toward civil rights legislation, while others have tampered with the administrative process so that civil rights legislation has changed in scope and emphasis.

Thomas Sowell, a Black economic policy advisor to Reagan, personifies this attitude. Sowell believes that culture, not discrimination, has set the Black race back in American society. Furthermore, Sowell advocates abolishing affirmative action, the minimum wage, and other government regulatory measures which historically have ensured a measure of equality.

The administration's stance on the Voting Rights Act again illustrates the changing scope of civil rights legislation. While almost all persons supported some form of the Voting Rights Act of 1965, many versions of the bill significantly diluted its power. The Reagan administration supported an amendment to the Section 5 preclearance proviso, which would have allowed jurisdictions with substantial records of compliance to "bail out" from under the act. While this may seem reasonable, the method for determining bail out was somewhat arbitrary.

Finally, important changes have taken place in government agencies that administer civil rights legislation. The EEOC has been left, for a substantial period of time, without commissioners or a chairperson. Those nominated for these positions have either questionable or deplorable civil rights records or lack the administrative ability to run such a large agency.

The Office of Federal Contract Compliance (OFCCP) has suffered drastic staff cuts, and new administrative guidelines on the number of contractors covered greatly limit the scope of its jurisdiction. Under the new guidelines, unless a contractor does $50,000 worth of business and has at least 100 employees, the employer would escape the inspection of OFCCP. This new provision allows the escape of literally thousands of contractors heretofore covered.

Business has traditionally fought government regulation in the workplace. One business attorney argued, "I think the pendulum has swung too far in favor of the employee. It is too easy for people to believe they have been discriminated against and use the Commission as a way to harass their employer. Business' fight against civil rights legislation is no different. The following are allegations made by business concerns against federal guidelines:

° Current Title VII Federal Law, OFCCP, and state civil rights laws place an expensive burden on businesses to defend themselves from non-meritorious claims of discrimination.

° The amount of paperwork, research, and record keeping that must be undertaken to meet government compliance is time-consuming, redundant, and expensive.

° Racism is being created, not deleted, by government-imposed "Affirmative Action Quotas" and guidelines on employee selection.

° Frivolous claims could be cut in half by shifting burdens of proof onto those who file charges.

° Employees only file charges to harass their former employers.

Increasingly, a two-tiered system of justice and access to justice is becoming apparent. While many of the notable achievements of the last two decades remain intact at the legislative level, at the administrative level -- the level of access and implementation -- there is disingegration and disrepair.

<u>WHAT STATES CAN DO</u>

<u>Stronger Civil Rights Laws</u>

° States should pass stronger civil rights legislation.
  These new, tougher, laws should serve to discourage employers from discriminating, and set tougher penalties
  for discrimination.

° States should strengthen state laws prohibiting discrimination in housing, employment and public accommodation.
  In these three areas, states must have self-initiatory
  powers (power to initiate a complaint without an aggrieved
  party filing a complaint).

° States should be allowed to seek punitive damages in discrimination cases, so that aggrieved parties can seek
  equitable remedy in both state and federal courts. Particularly in the areas of housing and public accommodation,
  existing state laws, for the most part, don't allow the
  types of remedial damages that would discourage such
  discrimination.

° States should broaden the umbrella of coverage in existing employment discrimination laws, to include small
  companies, large subcontractors and personnel placement
  agencies since they often contribute to employment discrimination.

° States should strengthen and incorporate into state civil
  service laws the mechanisms to address civil rights complaints through in-house grievance procedures. Inclusive
  in these procedures would be jurisdiction over unjust and
  discriminatory practices based upon race, sex, disability,
  age, national origin, and sexual harassment.

<u>State Civil Rights Agencies</u>

° States should increase funding and staffing of state and
  local civil rights agencies. Also the staff should be
  better trained to deal effectively with the business
  community in seeking compliance with existent laws.

<u>FOR FURTHER INFORMATION</u>

<u>Publications</u>

<u>Affirmative Action For the Handicapped</u>. A Handbook for Employment Opportunity Specialist of the Office of Federal Contract Compliance Programs, U.S. Department of Labor, Washington, D.C., April, 1980.

<u>Affirmative Action After Bakke</u>, Walter B. Connolly, Jr., Edmond J. Dilworth, Jr., Daniel E. Leach, 1978. Available from Law & Business, Inc., 757 Third Ave., New York, NY 10017.

<u>Dealing With Employment Discrimination</u>, Richard Peres, 1978, Available from McGraw-Hill Book Company, New York, NY.

Selected reports taken from <u>Labor Law Reports Employment Practices</u>, Commence Clearing House, Inc., 4025 W. Peterson Avenue, Chicago, IL 60646.

<u>Organizations</u>

CASH (Committee Against Sexual Harassment), 65 S. 4th St., Columbus, OH, 43215 (614) 224-9121.

OHIO GOVERNOR'S COMMITTEE ON EMPLOYMENT OF THE HANDICAPPED, 4656 Heaton Rd., Columbus, OH, 43229 (614) 466-8474.

NATIONAL ASSOCIATION FOR THE ADVANCEMENT OF COLORED PEOPLE, National Office, 1970 Broadway, New York, NY 10019.

NATIONAL ORGANIZATION FOR WOMEN, 425 13th St., N.W., Washington, D.C., 20004 (202) 347-2279, Eleanor Smeal, President.

NINE TO FIVE: A NATIONAL ORGANIZATION OF WORKING WOMEN, 1224 Huron Rd., Cleveland, OH, 44115 (216) 566-9308.

WOMEN'S NETWORK, 39 East Market, 5th Floor, Akron, OH, 44308 Kathy Stierhoff, Executive Director.

Prepared by Michael Samuels.

Women

BACKGROUND FACTS

The majority of women today are in the labor force. More than half of all children have working mothers.

Working women make less than men in every job at every educational level.

The median wage for all permanent, full-time women workers in 1980 was $11,220; for men it was $18,006; for women heading a household without a husband, $10,000.

The number of working women who are poor or "near poor" is large and growing. Most working women (three out of five) earn less than $10,000 a year. One out of three full-time working women earns less than $7,000.

35% of women workers are found in only 25 of 440 job categories. They work in sex-segregated occupational lines at rates of pay which do not equate comparable wages to comparable work.

There are now 8.2 million female-headed families, and the number is growing ten times as fast as male-headed families. Female headed households represent 15% of all families, but half of all poor families.

Women are on the lowest rungs of the economic ladder. Only 1% earn more than $25,000 per year.

Minority women face the double burden of race and sex discrimination. Women in general earn approximately 59 cents for every dollar earned by white men. Full-time black women workers, however, earn only about 54 cents, while Hispanic women earn only 49 cents.

Between 12 and 15 million women over the age of 35 are displaced homemakers; they are either divorced, widowed, or have been abandoned by their husbands.

Only ten states have Constitutional protection under the law for women. State inheritance taxes, tax law, and the property rights of husbands and wives discriminate against women.

<u>THE PROBLEM</u>

Women make up a majority of the population, yet until very recently their problems, needs and aspirations were ignored by federal, state, and local government. In the 1960s and 1970s a new sensitivity developed -- encouraged by the rising political power of the women's vote -- and a number of formal and informal barriers were broken down that prohibited women's full right to participate equally.

However, the conservative and traditional political forces that came to power with the election of Ronald Reagan in 1980 seem committed to reversing many of these gains. Most telling was the administration's role in preventing the ratification of the Equal Rights Amendment. Equally bad for women are the budget and program cutbacks presented by the administration to Congress.

The 1983 Reagan administration budget demands sacrifices for all, but the major burden of sacrifice falls on women. The budget cuts proposed by the President will have a devastating impact on women and their families at every stage of their lives.

Examined individually, the proposed cuts are harmful to women; in combination, the budget cuts are devastating. For example, not only are funds for training decreased, but child care support is being withdrawn; grants and loans for independent students are being cut; food programs for women, infants and school children are being eliminated. Each action diminishes opportunities for women and threatens the stability and health of the American family.

Women are increasingly important in the national workforce, and work and adequate income from work is increasingly important to women, their children, and their families. Women work, and they work in increasing numbers, but the pay they receive is all too frequently not comparable to the pay men receive for the same job.

In 1955 women made 64% as much as men; in 1980 women made 59% as much as men. During the 1960's both the Civil Rights Act and the Equal Employment Opportunities Act were passed. Obviously enactment of these two laws has had no effect on the widening wage differential. The reason for their impotence is the restrictive language in them and the unwillingness of the predominately male judiciary to broaden the interpretation.

Out of this dilemma has come a phrase which most leaders in women's issues feel will be the most pressing women's issue of the 1980's: equal pay for comparable worth. The comparable

worth theory holds that whole classes of jobs, such as clerical
positions, traditionally have been considered "women's work"
and have, as a result of this job segregation, been undervalued.

Historical reasons for this undervaluation of women's
jobs are complex. Those opposed to the idea of comparable
worth blame women's "temporary" status in the workforce. She
works until she marries, or, if married, she works to maintain
a standard of living or to help out.

Another argument is that pay for a job is determined in
the marketplace. Although in most communities there exists a
shortage of both secretaries and registered nurses, salaries
have not risen appreciably for either profession. In fact,
in a comparable worth suit brought against the city and county
of Denver by city-county nurses, it was pointed out that
intensive care nurses make less than tree trimmers, painters
or tire-service men. The nurses lost the court case when the
judge ruled that their claim was "pregnant with the possibility
of disrupting the entire economic system of the United States."

A major reason such disparity is allowed to continue in
this country is that biased or dual classification systems
are allowed to be used to measure job worth. Tasks and conditions found primarily in men's jobs are given more compens-
atory weight than tasks and conditions found predominately
in women's jobs.

The majority of women in the labor force or out are
not "comfortable." Most are struggling to keep their heads
above water and to provide the basic needs (food, clothing
and shelter) for their families.

Many of these women -- known as the "working poor" --
are confronting a difficult decision. If they stay in the
workforce and continue to strive toward self-sufficiency,
under Reagan regulations they will soon be unable to qualify
for benefits which protect their families from illness,
malnutrition, etc. The only real option for many is to leave
the workforce and become totally dependent on public financial
assistance, Medicaid, and food stamps.

Also, many women are not in the workforce. Millions of
middle-aged and elderly women are separated, divorced, or
widowed. They dedicated most of their lives to the role of
homemaker. They have skills which are valuable but rarely
seen as marketable. They have responsibility for themselves
and often for dependent children. With a low percentage
receiving alimony, pensions, survivor's benefits or inherited
wealth, they have few choices. Age discrimination in the
marketplace then compounds the problems experienced by these
displaced homemakers.

WHAT STATES CAN DO

Pay Equity

° States should enact legislation mandating the state civil
  service department to evaluate the state workforce with
  regard to occupational segregation, broken down by race and
  sex, the skills required for each occupation, the level of
  compensation, and develop a report with recommended changes
  in categories, skill requirements, and salary levels in
  order to acheive pay equity.

Removing Economic Bias

° States should pass legislation requiring insurance companies
  to use only single sex tables in determining premiums and
  benefits.

° States should require state and local public employee pension funds to give divorced spouses property rights in
  any pension benefits after 10 years of married life.

Children and Child Care

° States should enact legislation developing comprehensive
  programs for maternal and child health including health
  maintenance, immunization and nutrition to make up for
  cutbacks in those federal programs.

° States should create a special Blue Ribbon Commission to
  survey the child care needs of the state, propose concrete
  recommendations to meet the child care needs of state
  employees, and to meet the child care needs of the private
  sector.

Education

° States should require the State Department of Education
  to develop bias free curriculum and textbooks for introduction throughout school systems in the state.

Constitutional Amendments

° States should amend their own state constitutions to include the Equal Rights Amendment.

° States should ratify the federal Equal Rights Amendment,
  when it passes Congress and is submitted to the states
  for ratification.

° States should oppose ratification of any federal constitutional amendment that would give the states or Congress the
  right to limit or prohibit abortions.

<u>FOR FURTHER INFORMATION</u>

<u>Publications</u>

<u>Equal Pay for Work of Comparable Worth: An Annotated
Bibliography of the Business and Professional Women's Foundation.</u>
American Library Association, 50 Eash Huron Street, Chicago,
IL 60611 (312) 944-6780.

<u>Inequality of Sacrifice: The Impact of the Reagan Budget
on Women</u>, National Education Association, 1201 Sixteenth
St., N.W., Washington, DC 20036 (202) 833-4000.

<u>Manual on Pay Equity, Raising Wages for Women's Work</u>,
$9.95 from the Conference on Alternative State and Local
Policies, 2000 Florida Ave., N.W., Washington, DC 20009
(202) 387-6030.

<u>The Spirit of Houston, The First National Women's Con-
ference</u>, March, 1978, National Commission on the Observance
of International Women's Year, U. S. Government Printing
Office., Washington, DC 20402.

"...To Form a More Perfect Union...," Justice for
<u>American Women</u>, Report of the National Commission on the
Observance of International Women's Year, 1976. U. S. Government Printing Office, Washington, DC 20402.

<u>Organizations</u>

NATIONAL COMMITTEE ON PAY EQUITY, 1201 16th Street, NW,
Suite 615, Washington, D.C. 20036 (202) 822-7304.
Joy Ann Grune, Director.

NATIONAL COMMISSION ON WORKING WOMEN, 2000 P Street, NW,
#508, Washington, DC 20036 (202) 872-1782. Sandra Porter,
Executive Director.

NATIONAL WOMEN'S POLITICAL CAUCUS, 1411 K Street, NW, #1110.
Washington, DC 20005 (202) 347-4456. Carol Bros.

NINE TO FIVE: A NATIONAL ORGANIZATION OF WORKING WOMEN,
1224 Huron Road, Cleveland, OH 44115 (216) 566-9308. Karen
Nussbaum.

WOMEN'S EQUITY ACTION LEAGUE, 805 15th Street, NW, Suite
822, Washington, DC 20005 (202) 638-1961. Pat Reuss,
Legislative Director.

WOMEN'S LEGAL DEFENSE FUND, 2000 P Street, NW, Washington,
D.C. 20036 (202) 887-0364. Judith Lichtman, Executive Director.

Prepared by Linda Tarr-Whelan

Crime

Criminal Justice

BACKGROUND FACTS

Violent crime in the United States represents a continuing social disaster unmatched in the developed world.

By the late 1970's, an American's chances of being murdered were about ten times those of a Swede, West German, or Japanese, fifteen times those of an Englishman or a Swiss, and twenty times those of a Dane.

Thirty-four out of every thousand Americans were the victims of some violent crime in 1979.

Moreover, though the threat of criminal violence crosses all social, economic, and geographic boundaries, it is much more severe for some groups, and in some places, than others. It is much more an urban problem than a rural or suburban one, much more threatening to the young than to the middle-aged and elderly, much more a pervasive fact of life for the poor and minority than for the affluent and white.

And though no state has been spared the fear and anguish that serious crime brings, the scale of the problem is different across different states; different in New York, for example, where the homicide rate is about 13 per 100,000 per year, than in Vermont, where the rate is about just over 2 per 100,000

It is widely believed, both by the public and by elected officials, that crime has increased drastically in the last few years; that, as Newsweek magazine put it in 1981, we are suffering an "epidemic" of violent crime. Problems of reporting and measuring crime make precise estimates of trends over time difficult. Yet the evidence suggests that, nationally, rates of serious violent crime probably leveled off during the mid-1970's and increased somewhat thereafter, with some crimes (including murder) possibly declining in 1981 and others (including robbery) apparently still increasing.

Violent crime takes an enormous toll -- not only in injuries and death, but also in pervasive and often crippling fear in many communities and in the massive diversion of scarce public resources into police, courts, and prisons.

State governments alone spent almost $4.5 billion on corrections in 1980 -- more than they spent on all natural resources programs, more than twice what they spent on employment security, and more than ten times what they spent on corrections in 1960.

<u>THE PROBLEM</u>

In the last several years, most legislative initiatives against crime have emphasized "getting tough" with criminals. States have adopted stiff, mandatory sentences for repeat offenders or those who use weapons, have provided for even very young criminals to be tried in adult criminal courts; and (as in New York) have established harsh penalties for drug offenses.

The most dramatic expression of this mood has been the recent passage in California of a "Victim's Bill of Rights" (Proposition 8) that mandates a wide range of major changes in criminal justice policy. Proposition 8's provisions ranged from the abolition of felony plea-bargaining, to heavy restrictions on the right to bail, to a vague provision enforcing the right of children to attend "safe" schools.

These "get tough" policy initiatives have been based on two related arguments. The first, and most common, is that American criminal justice is "soft" on criminals -- crimes are committed because the "costs" of committing a crime have gone down drastically. The second is that, there is little government can do to reduce crime rates. Programs to rehabilitate offenders, in this view, are uniformly failures, and the experience of the 1960's "proves" that such measures as employment and training programs and antipoverty efforts cannot prevent crime.

Though few people would disagree that we need an efficient and effective criminal justice system, the premise that our current system is dramatically weak -- and that we can stop crime by getting still "tougher" -- is wrong. The harsher policies of the past several years, in fact, must be seen as an experiment that has largely failed.

By September, 1981, the state and federal prison population stood at an all-time high of 357,000 -- up an astonishing 82% since 1970, and up by 30,000 from the start of 1981 alone. Yet this dramatic increase has had no discernible effect on rates of serious crime. In California, the rate of first commitments of young men to the state's Youth Authority rose 55% from 1972 to 1980; but California's robbery rate continues to rise.

The United States now imprisons its population at a rate of about 150 per 100,000 -- far greater than any comparable industrial society (except two with huge populations of political prisoners -- the Soviet Union and South Africa). The Dutch rate of imprisonment, in the late 1970's, was <u>18</u> per 100,000. Yet our rates of serious violent crime remain <u>far</u> higher.

Some of the states with the highest rates of imprisonment -with the highest "costs" of crime -- are also those
with some of the highest rates of serious violent crime.
Georgia imprisons people at a rate about six times that of
New Hampshire, and has more than four times New Hampshire's
homicide rate. North Carolina has five times the imprisonment
rate of Minnesota and four times the murder rate. New York's
imprisonment rate is more than double the rate in Massachusetts,
and it has triple the murder rate. Nevada has both the
highest imprisonment rate and the highest murder rate of any
state in the union excluding the District of Columbia.

In general -- though some particular jurisdictions may
be excessively lenient with offenders -- the failure of the
criminal justice system to deal sharply with "hard-core" or
"career" offenders is not the main problem. Sometimes,
these criminals do "fall through the cracks" of the justice
system -- but not often. Several studies have found, for
example, that repeat violent offenders have about a 9 in 10
chance of imprisonment once convicted in the jurisdictions
studied. A major evaluation of special "career criminal"
programs -- designed to give prosecutors more resources to
deal more effectively with repeat offenders -- found that
the programs had unexpectedly small effects, because the
prosecutors were already doing a good job of putting repeat
offenders away. (The often relatively lax treatment of
family violence -- especially of men who assault their wives
-- is a frequent exception to this general point.)

The much more significant problem is that most crimes do
not even result in an arrest. One RAND Corporation study of
repeat felons in California found that their chances of being
arrested for any one robbery were about one in ten. To change
this pattern significantly, we would need to develop dramatically more effective police strategies; but despite considerable
research no one has yet come up with those strategies.

All of this means that crime prevention must be once
again given a high priority on state and local agendas.
Several years ago, it was widely believed that programs to
prevent crime in the community and to rehabilitate offenders
had failed. Today the picture is more encouraging. Though
there is much still to be learned, we know more about what
might prevent crime than some have argued. And though some
of the measures we could take are long-term ones -- like
achieving full and rewarding employment, and controlling the
economic forces that tend to disrupt and fragment families
and local communities -- others are within the range of more
immediate policy.

WHAT STATES CAN DO

Community Prevention

° States should develop and evaluate local community dispute
  resolution mechanisms, typified by San Francisco's Community
  Boards program, which trains local people to mediate disputes
  among neighbors, family members, and others.

° States should develop programs to link employment, training,
  and education programs for offenders and high-risk youth
  with broader strategies of locally-based economic development.
  The most promising long-run strategy against crime involves
  local development programs that can help maintain crucial
  family and community networks while offering the realistic
  chance of stable, long-term employment.

° States should promote "neighborhood watch" programs to encourage community residents to become involved in anti-crime
  programs. Although the effectiveness of these programs is
  not certain, Detroit reports a 30% drop in crime in
  areas with neighborhood watches.

Family Interventions

° States should support the development of comprehensive
  family service programs, exemplified by the Child and Family
  Resource Programs piloted by HEW in the 1970's. Research
  consistently shows that violent crime is associated with
  childhood experiences in abusive or highly stressed families.

° States should help establish, fund, and provide technical
  assistance to family violence reduction programs both within
  and outside of local criminal justice systems. Sixteen
  percent of homicides in 1980 involved family relationships;
  half of them were spouse killings.

Programs for Offenders

° States should develop programs to provide adequate financial
  assistance to released prisoners. Federally-sponsored
  experiments in Maryland, Georgia and Texas have shown that
  post-release stipends can have a major impact on recidivism,
  for violent as well as property crimes.

° States should develop "supported work" programs for offenders,
  addicts, and other "high risk" groups. These programs,
  pioneered in New York by the Vera Foundation, offer a carefully structured work program with gradually increasing
  rewards and responsibilities and a variety of support
  services.

<u>FOR FURTHER INFORMATION</u>

<u>Publications</u>

   <u>American Prisons and Jails</u>, Joan Mullen, et al, 1980.
U.S. Department of Justice, National Institute of Justice,
Washington, D.C. A thorough analysis of trends in imprisonment
and the options for reducing prison crowding.

   <u>Citizen Crime Prevention Tactics: A Literature Review
and Selected Bibliography</u>, U.S. Department of Justice, National
Institute of Justice, Washington, D.C., 1980. Useful review of
various kinds of prevention programs and the studies of their
effectiveness.

   <u>Criminal Justice Abstracts</u>, National Council on Crime and
Delinquency, Hackensack, N.J. 07601. Quarterly abstracts of
literature from a variety of publications concerned with crime
and criminal justice. Invaluable as a quick, guide to current
research and debates.

   <u>Deterrence and Incapacitation: Estimating the Effects of
Criminal Sanctions on Crime Rates</u>, Alfred Blumstein, Jacqueline
Cohen, and Daniel Nagin; National Academy of Sciences, Washington,
D.C., 1978. Technical, but extremely important, analyses of
the effects of increasing crime's "costs."

   <u>Summary and Findings of the National Supported Work
Demonstration</u>, Manpower Demonstration Research Corporation,
Cambrige, MA, Ballinger Press, 1980. Careful description and
analysis of supported work experiments.

<u>Organizations</u>

CALIFORNIA COMMISSION ON CRIME CONTROL AND VIOLENCE PREVENTION,
9719 Lincoln Village Drive, Suite 600, Sacramento, CA 95827
(916) 366-5338. An example of a state-level research and advocacy
commission. Has published a report, <u>An Ounce of Prevention</u>,
examining literature on causes and prevention of crime.

NATIONAL COUNCIL ON CRIME AND DELINQUENCY, Continental Plaza,
411 Hackensack Ave., Hackensack, N.J. 07601. National
organization of concerned criminal justice professionals,
researchers and citizens. Publishes a journal, <u>Crime and
Delinquency</u>, as well as quarterly <u>Criminal Justice Abstracts</u>.

NATIONAL MORATORIUM ON PRISON CONSTRUCTION, Unitarian Univers-
alist Service Committee, 1251 Second Ave., San Francisco, CA
94122 (415) 731-3300. Provides information on problems and
costs of incarceration and on alternatives to imprisonment.

Prepared by Elliot Currie.

Handgun Control

The statistics of handgun violence in America are appall-
ing. In 1980, 11,522 Americans were murdered with handguns,
2.5 times more often than with any other weapon. That figure
represents 50% of all the murders in America that year.
On an average day, 32 Americans are murdered with handguns.

In 1980 51% of handgun murders were perpetrated by
relatives or persons acquainted with their victims. Of these
murders, 16% were within families, half of which involved
spouse killing spouse. Forty-five percent of all murders in
1980 were the result of arguments, while 18% occurred as a
result of felonious activities such as robbery or rape.

There are an estimated 50-60 million handguns in Amerca,
and almost 2.5 million new handguns are put into circulation
every year. At the current rate of production, the American
handgun population will be 100 million by the year 2000.

During the Vietnam War, more than 40,000 American soldiers
were killed in action. During that same period, more than
50,000 American civilians were murdered here in the United
States with handguns.

Because of its concealable and lethal nature, the handgun
is clearly the favorite weapon of criminals. According to
FBI statistics for 1980, handguns were used in some 220,000
robberies and 157,000 aggravated assaults in that year. One
in nine Americans has been threatened or attacked by someone
wielding a handgun.

In 1979, handguns were used to kill 48 people in Japan,
8 in Great Britain, 34 in Switzerland, 52 in Canada, 58 in
Israel, 21 in Sweden, 42 in West Germany, and 10,728 in the
United States. Unlike the United States, these other Western
nations have tough handgun control laws.

More important than all the statistics of handgun violence
are the lives they represent. "The victims of the violence
are black and white, rich and poor, young and old, famous and
unknown," said Robert Kennedy in 1968, just two months before
he himself was to become a victim of handgun violence. "They
are most important of all, human beings whom other human
beings loved and needed. No one -- no matter where he lives
or what he does -- can be certain who next will suffer from
some senseless act of bloodshed. And yet it goes on and on
in this country of ours. Why?"

Six major arguments are raised by the gun lobby to oppose handgun control legislation:

"The Second Amendment guarantees individuals the right to keep and bear arms." In fact, the Second Amendment to the U.S. Constitution does not guarantee such a right to individuals. The Second Amendment reads in full: "A Well Regulated Militia Being Necessary to the Security of a Free State, the Right of the People to Keep and Bear Arms Shall Not Be Infringed."

On five separate occasions, the U.S. Supreme Court has ruled that the Second Amendment was intended to protect members of a state militia from being disarmed by the federal government. In addition, the American Bar Association has stated that "every Federal Court decision involving the amendment has given the amendment a collective, militia interpretation and/or held that firearms control laws enacted under a state's police power are constitutional."

In the past year, there have been three significant court decisions upholding the rights of states and localities to control handguns. The Ohio Supreme Court has upheld one community's laws requiring a special weapon owners' identification card, and the U.S. District Court has ruled the Morton Grove, Illinois restrictive handgun ordinance is constitutional. A Rhode Island law requiring handgun purchasers to obtain a safety certificate has been upheld by the U.S. District Court as a reasonable way to promote handgun safety.

"Gun control will leave citizens defenseless from criminals." Under federal legislation proposed by Senator Edward Kennedy and Congressman Peter Rodino (the Kennedy-Rodino Handgun Crime Control Bill), law-abiding citizens will still have no difficulty getting handguns. Even so, citizens should think twice before getting a handgun for self-protection. Statistics show clearly that a handgun kept for self-defense is far more dangerous to its owner and his family than it is to the criminal. For example, California statistics show that if you purchase a gun it is over 11 times as likely to be used to kill you, your spouse, or your children as it is to kill an intruder in your home.

"When guns are outlawed, only outlaws will have guns." This is one of the simplest -- and most popular -- slogans of the gun lobby. Under any realistic federal control of handguns (such as the Kennedy-Rodino Bill), law-abiding citizens will still be able to buy handguns, but it will be more difficult for criminals to get them. Furthermore, rifles and shotguns will not be affected at all by any handgun control legislation.

"Handgun control is the first step toward confiscation of all guns." Public opinion polls show what type of handgun control the American people want. A July, 1981 Gallup poll showed that 91% of the American people favor a three-week waiting period with a background check for handgun purchases. Handgun control is just handgun control -- not rifle control or shotgun control.

The United States is a democratic nation, and under the democratic process, laws will be passed to give the American people what they want, not what they don't want. Those in the gun lobby who compare the United States to Hitler's Germany or Communist regimes apparently have little faith in our democratic system.

"Guns don't kill, people do." People do kill people, but they do so mostly with handguns. The handgun is a weapon designed and made for the purpose of killing human beings, and it is more lethal than any other murder weapon. It is used 2 1/2 times more often than any other murder weapon.

"People also kill people with automobiles," Pete Shields, Chairman of Handgun Control, Inc. recently wrote, "and thus we regulate their use, but the many local, state, and national car clubs do not bombard Congress and the public with appeals for the unregulated use of cars and trucks."

We regulate all kinds of other dangerous substances in our country. Drugs, for example, are strictly regulated, and those who dispense them must be licensed. Some drugs, such as heroin, are considered so lethal that they are banned entirely.

"Control criminals, not guns." It is true that we should do something to control criminals -- and one way is by controlling handguns, the criminals' favorite weapon. Admittedly, there are other things which need to be done to improve our criminal justice system -- prison reform and rehabilitation, judicial sentencing and parole,and a host of other solutions. We should put the criminals behind bars, but while we're doing that, we should also take preventive measures. Handgun control is one way to make it more difficult for criminals to get their favorite tool -- the deadly, concealable handgun.

<u>WHAT STATES CAN DO</u>

States should enact handgun control laws based on one of the three following models:

<u>Mandatory Sentences for Carrying Unlicensed Handguns</u>

A Massachusetts law passed in 1975 is the toughest handgun control law in the country. Called the Bartley-Fox law, it requires a one-year mandatory minimum prison term for anyone caught carrying a handgun without a license outside his home or place of business.

Not only is the law tough, but effective. A study of the law's impact by the Center for Applied Social Research at Northeastern University in Boston showed that between 1974 and 1976, gun homicides in Boston declined 43% compared to 11.1% for other cities of similar size; gun-related armed robberies dropped 35.1% in Massachusetts compared to 11.7% in the rest of the country; and gun assaults declined by 19.3% in Massachusetts while dropping only 4.2% in the rest of the country.

<u>Registration of Firearms and Freezing Handgun Sales</u>

A law passed in 1977 in the District of Columbia required the registration of all currently owned handguns, rifles, and shotguns, and froze the number of legal handguns by banning the sale or possession of additional handguns by private citizens. A study of that law by Edward D. Jones III, a former analyst for the Justice Department, compared statistics in the District of Columbia for 1974 and 1978 (the first full year after the law went into effect), which showed that family killings caused by handgun abuse decreased from 10% in 1974 to 5% in 1978, and handgun homicides among neighbors, lovers, and other nonfamily acquaintances dropped from 44% to 38%.

<u>Handgun Registration, Freezing Handgun Sales and Prohibiting
    Mail Order Sales</u>

The major activity for handgun control at the state level this year is taking place in California. An initiative on the state ballot this November would, if passed: 1) require registration of all handguns in the state within one year after passage of the initiative; 2) not allow the sale of registered handguns until 18 months after passage of the initiative, thus putting a lid on the number of handguns in California; require a mandatory six-month jail sentence for carrying a concealed, unregistered handgun; and 4) prohibit mail orders of concealable firearms at once.

Publications

Guns Don't Die, People Do, by Pete Shields, Chairman of
Handgun Control, Inc. Available at your local bookstore or
order for $6.95 (price includes postage and handling) from
Arbor House Publishing Company, 235 E. 45th St., New York,
NY, 10017. This recently published book presents the case
for handgun control, including an explanation of current gun
laws and legislation before Congress. It provides shocking
facts about handguns and what can and must be done about
them.

Federal Regulation of Firearms, a report prepared by the
Congressional Research Service of the Library of Congress for
the Senate Judiciary Committee. Available for sale from the
Superintendent of Documents, U.S. Government Printing Office,
Washington, D.C. 20402. This government document provides a
summation of major congressional legislation and of state
handgun control laws.

The Snub-Nosed Killers: Handguns in America, a series
of articles which appeared in the Cox newspapers in fall
1981. This award-winning series presents evidence that
handguns with a barrel-length of three inches or less are
the most favored weapons of criminals.

Organizations

HANDGUN CONTROL, INC., 810 18th St., N.W., Washington, D.C.
20006 (202) 638-4723. Works with state and local handgun
control groups; will provide information on how to contact a
group in your state or community.

NATIONAL COALITION TO BAN HANDGUNS, 100 Maryland Ave, NE
Washington, DC 20002 (202) 544-7190. Lobbies Congress and
works on the state and local levels to ban possession of handguns.

Prepared by Donald Fraher

Education

Public Education

America's system of public education is entering a critical period.

Maintaining and expanding our public school system in the midst of massive cuts in federal assistance, a deepening economic recession, and strong citizen opposition to higher state and local taxes will be a difficult task.

Cutbacks in federal education programs will hurt the quality of education in schools across the country. While local districts only receive on the average about 8 percent of their funds from federal programs, those programs are critical because they concentrate on assistance to the disadvantaged, the disabled, and the needy.

The states' role in financing education is growing more important. In the 1981-82 school year, for example, states contributed nearly half of all public school revenues, local sources 43 percent and the federal government roughly 8 percent.

States and local school districts face difficult problems picking up the burden of federal cuts, and maintaining funding for their existing programs.

States surpluses have fallen from $11 billion in 1980 to $4.7 billion in 1981. Remaining surpluses are concentrated in 12 energy-producing states. During 1982 state spending is expected to exceed state revenue by $5 billion.

In addition, state and local governments are faced with pressure from a variety of sources to pick up programs eliminated from the federal budget. For example, staggering new demands to rehabilitate state and local infrastructure (for example, bridges, roads, dams and ports) will compete with education and other human services programs.

States vary widely in the amount, and kind of education they provide. The amount of financial assistance, the requirements established for students and teachers, and the standards of quality can be as different as night and day from one state to the next. On the average, states spend $378.85 per capita on education. But Alaska spends $1,105, while Tennessee spends only $280.

<u>THE PROBLEM</u>

The founders of this nation were indeed wise when they
made the education of the nation's citizens a national imperative. They saw it as a most effective tool in the development
of basic skills required in the building of a nation, and
the means to meet the need for a skilled and educated workforce.

Our classrooms, school libraries and laboratories are,
after all, critical institutions. At their best, they not
only train the minds of our children and hone their skills but
they are also powerful institutions advancing our health, our
safety, our economic well-being, our common defense, our rights
and our freedoms. They enrich the nation's culture. They
inculcate the ideals and the value systems of our democracy.
They inspire commonality of purpose.

The federal role in education has increased over the
years to meet national priorities, such the National Defense
Education Act in 1958, or the passage of the GI "Bill of
Rights". However, at no time has that federal aid averaged
more than 8 per cent of all education expenditures in the
country.

But with the advent of the Reagan administration, this
vital aid is threatened. In his FY 1983 budget, President
Reagan proposed paring a third from the federal education
budget. While Congressional intervention spared some cuts,
massive decreases have been made in many programs. Chapter
I, Bilingual education, Education for the Handicapped, Impact
Aid: all have been cut, kept at FY '82 levels, or given
only slight increases.

Thoughtful conservatives are expressing misgivings
about a diminished public investment in education. Denis P.
Doyle of the American Enterprise Institute, for instance,
described the cutbacks in higher education spending as unwise
public policy when no workable alternative is proposed by
the Reagan administration. Failure to invest in the education
of doctors, physicists, mathematicians and engineers, he
says, will mean those skills will not be there to meet our
future needs. "It takes 20 years to train the next generation
of engineers, scientists and linguists," he notes.

The current economic recession, huge slashes in federally-
supported social programs, including education, and federal
tax cuts have hit states hard. These measures have had a
profound effect on the financial capabilities of states and
cities to maintain, let alone expand, existing commitments
to social programs without huge tax increases.

One of the main goals in federal education programs has
been to ensure equity of access to education for all the
nation's citizens. But those federal programs are now being
systematically dismantled or cut back. Translated into
human terms, these losses in funding mean literally hundreds
of thousands of young people denied the opportunity to better
prepare themselves for the future.

The term "tax revolt" has received wide national attention
in recent years, as citizens in city after city and state
after state "rebelled" by voting in measures limiting local
government's power of taxation.

This greater financial responsibility of the states
will mean that state political leaders will be facing harder
choices. Allocations for vital functions such as bridge and
road repair will come into direct competition with funding
for social and human service programs such as welfare, food
stamps and education. While it is clear that infrastructure
needs must be met, legislators cannot lose sight of the fact
that education is also an investment in the future of the
state, and indeed of the country.

Despite these difficult choices, state legislators must
keep quality education for all students throughout their
state as a top priority. States and local school districts
facing bleak financial futures may tend to turn back the
clock on progressive moves aimed at equalizing per pupil
expenditures and closing the disparities between wealthy and
poor school districts. States should aim for a high quality
education for all students regardless of the wealth of their
particular school district.

In addition, at the same time that the administration
is proposing huge cutbacks in federal education assistance,
it is proposing a boondoggle for the nation's wealthy and
upper middle-classes, and its private schools in the form of
the tuition tax credit scheme. If this passes it would be a
powerful role model for state statutes as well.

Similarly, voucher plans, proposed on and off for several
decades now, would extend the public funding of schools to
include parochial and private schools by allowing parents of
elementary and secondary school children to use their voucher
-- worth a designated amount -- in a private, parochial or
public school.

WHAT STATES CAN DO

Maintain Adequate Funding and Equity

° States should maintain and expand programs that attempt to
  equalize the funding availability for all districts so that
  students in poorer areas will have the same access to
  quality education as students in wealthier districts.

° States should maintain and expand programs that provide
  equity of access and, when necessary, remedial assistance
  to minority and disadvantaged students.

° States should maintain and expand education and rehabilitation programs for the handicapped.

° States should maintain and expand vocational and adult
  education programs.

Collective Bargaining

° States should enact legislation guaranteeing the right of
  collective bargaining to teachers and other employees
  in the state's public school systems.

Teacher Education

° States should continue and expand adequate funding for
  teacher training and education programs at state colleges
  and universities.

° States should provide adequate funding for programs of
  continuing education for teachers.

Tuition Tax Credits

° States should defeat legislation that would provide tuition
  tax credits for students attending private schools.

Voucher Plan

° States should defeat legislation that would create educational
  "voucher" plans because they would fatally weaken America's
  public school system.

<u>FOR FURTHER INFORMATION</u>

<u>Publications:</u>

<u>The Federal Education Budget, An NEA Policy Paper</u>,
NEA Governmental Relations, 1201 Sixteenth Street, NW,
Washington, DC 20036, 202-822-7300. This publication analyzes
the impact of federal budget priorities and the new federalism
on education.

<u>The Federal Role in Education, An NEA Policy Paper</u>,
This paper traces the history of the Federal role in education,
explains the rationale for it, and discusses the wisdom of
maintaining a Cabinet department.

<u>Rankings of the States, 1981</u>, National Education Asso-
ciation, Research Department, 1201 16th St.,N.W., Washington,
D.C., 20036.

<u>1981 Annual Report</u>, Advisory Panel on Financing Elementary
and Secondary Education, P.O. Box 19125, Washington, D.C.,
20036.

<u>Organizations</u>

AMERICAN FEDERATION OF TEACHERS, 11 Dupont Circle, N.W.,
Washington, D.C., 20036 (202) 797-4400. An excellent source
for information on problems affecting public education.

EDUCATION COMMISSION OF THE STATES, 1860 Lincoln St., Denver,
CO, 80295 (303) 830-3785. E.C.S. works with state political
and educational leaders to improve policies in education,
and serves as a clearinghouse for policies and proposals on
educational reform.

NATIONAL ASSOCIATION OF STATE BOARDS OF EDUCATION, 444 North
Capitol St., Room 256, Washington, D.C., 20001 (202) 624-5845.
N.A.S.B.E. provides information to members on governmental
activity vis a vis education, and prints special projects
publications on educational problems of the gifted, talented,
handicapped, and the underprivileged.

NATIONAL EDUCATION ASSOCIATION, 1201 16th Street, N.W.,
Washington, D.C., 20036 (202) 822-7300. NEA is an excellent
source for information on problems affecting public education.

Prepared by Linda Tarr-Whelan.

Students

Nearly 12 million postsecondary students attend some
3200 colleges, universities, two-year, professional and technical schools. They can be found in virtually every congressional and legislative district in the country. Eight
states (California, Florida, Illinois, Massachusetts, Michigan,
Ohio, New York and Texas) have student populations of 400,000
or more.

In addition to postsecondary students, some 18 million
people - nearly 12 per cent of the adult population--partic-
ipate in some form of adult education. As the notion of
"lifelong learning" becomes widespread, more adults will be
turning to colleges and universities to gain job retraining,
new job skills and further intellectual development.

Educational opportunities for economically disadvantaged
students increased dramatically in the 1960s and 1970s, made
possible, to a large extent, by expansion of federal financial
assistance programs. By 1980, over four million students
received aid from three need-based federal programs -- more
than three times the number of recipients just six years earlier.
Access to higher education, however, is severely threatened
by the Reagan administration's slashes in funding for financial
assistance.

In contrast to their counterparts in the 1960s, students
today are often portrayed as apathetic or conservative. While
campuses are certainly not the hotbeds of political activity
they were 15 years ago, student activism is still alive and
strong. Using check-off systems on university registration
forms, students have funded stable, professionally-staffed
nonprofit organizations to represent their interests and to
expand educational opportunities beyond the classroom.

Public Interest Research Groups (PIRGs), which conduct
research, lobbying and organizing on consumer issues, can be
found on over 120 campuses in 20 states. State Student Associations (SSAs) lobby legislatures for student interests, especially on financial aid questions. Numerous states, including
California, New York and Pennsylvania, boast influential
student lobbies.

<u>THE PROBLEM</u>

While no overriding issues dominate college campuses as civil rights and Vietnam did in the 1960s, several issues are important to large numbers of students.

<u>Financial Aid</u>   Perhaps foremost among student concerns is the question of whether students can attend college at all. Almost half of all students receive some form of government financial aid. Yet the Reagan administration has reversed the long-standing American commitment to provide a college education to any qualified person, regardless of income. According to the American Council on Education, the President's proposed FY 1983 budget cuts would:

° Eliminate over one million disadvantaged students from the Pell Grant program and reduce the maximum grant to $1600.

° Drop all graduate and professional students from eligibility for the Guaranteed Student Loan program and double the origination fee. Five hundred thousand to a million students would be eliminated from the program.

° Slash funding for the TRIO programs for disadvantaged students by nearly half and drop 250,000 jobs from the College Work Study program

° Eliminate funding for National Direct Student Loans and Supplemental Educational Opportunity Grants (both of which aid needy students) and State Student Incentive Grants. The loss of SSIGs, which match state student financial aid grants, would be particularly damaging to states. Fifteen states currently count on SSIGs for 50% of their grant programs.

College costs are currently rising 15 to 20 per cent. The average cost of attending a public university is almost $4,000 annually, private college costs average $7,000 per year. These escalating costs have forced many colleges to reverse long-held policies of admitting students regardless of financial need. Students, too, have been obliged to change their college plans, based on financial considerations. A <u>Cronicle of Higher Education</u> study of fall 1981 enrollments found that some student who would have preferred private colleges are attending state universities; students who might have gone to state universities are opting for community colleges.

According to the <u>Los Angeles Times</u>, "Because of the worsening budget problems on the local level, few state legislatures are able to fill the gap left by the federal cuts." In fact, many states have raised their tuition and room and board fees to meet budgetary problems.

Student financial aid opponents traditionally raise two
arguments. First, they argue, in the words of David Stockman,
that "if people want to go to college bad enough, then there's
opportunity and responsibility on their part to finance their
way the best they can." These critics don't explain how millions
of students can find adequately-paying jobs when the adult unemployment rate is the worst since 1941; teenage unemployment
in some areas exceeds 50 per cent; and a quarter of a million
jobs have been eliminated from the College Work Study program.

Financial aid critics, including the conservative Heritage
Foundation, also maintain that government has no obligation to
aid students, since, in their view, education is more a private
than a public benefit. This argument ignores the crucial importance of a well-educated population to a modern, technological
society. If the U.S. is to compete effectively in the world
economy, it must have skilled, trained citizens. Though Japan
has only half our population, it currently graduates 50% more
students with engineering degrees. Despite the proliferation
of computers throughout American society, the U.S. graduates
fewer doctorates in computer science than we did in the mid-
1970s.

<u>Other Concerns</u> Students face other barriers in their
path to higher education. Lack of campus child care facilities
keeps women and disadvantaged students from attending college.
Federal programs ensuring equal opportunity to women (Title
IX) and disabled students (Section 504) have been neglected or
opposed by the Reagan administration.

Participation in university decision-making and control
of student fees are also major student concerns. In many
states students are denied voting representation on state
university boards of trustees. Students have also been denied
the right to control their fee systems and to voluntarily tax
themselves to fund student-run, nonprofit organizations.

Finally, students face discrimination in their roles as
citizens. Some localities prevent students from voting in
their college communiites; students are, in many cases, exempted
from minimum wage protections; and landlords may discriminate
against students seeking off-campus housing (such as prohibiting more than three unrelated people from living under the
same roof).

State policies should guarantee students the same rights
granted to other citizens. With the Reagan administration's
abdication of the federal role in higher education, states
must also take action to ensure the right of any qualified
person to higher education. In the 1980s the decisions of
state policy-makers will determine whether America has the
well-educated population essential to both the national
economy and a democratic society.

WHAT STATES CAN DO

Ensuring Equal Access to Education

° States should set up low-interest loan or grant programs for
  students. Rhode Island is using bonds to fund a new $100
  million loan program. This fall Illinois will launch a
  loan program for private college students. Other states
  considering student loan legislation include Florida,
  Iowa, Kentucky, Maryland, Minnesota, and Pennsylvania.

  States should also investigate the use of public pension
  funds to support loan or grant programs for children of public
  employees.

° States should establish programs to fund campus child care
  services and, where necessary, require schools to provide
  services to help disadvantaged students. These services
  should be available at night for part-time students.
  California's Campus Child Care Development Act supports
  child care at public and private institutions. The state
  has also directed public vocational colleges to give special
  child care services to students to aid them in surmounting
  social and economic obstacles to education.

° States should pass legislation equivalent to the federal
  Title IX program to protect educational opportunities for
  women from federal neglect. Alaska and Nebraska are among
  the states with "mini Title IX" programs.

Protecting Student Rights

° States should legally recognize the right of students to
  control their own fees; the Wisconsin law is the best model.
  States should reject legislation prohibiting the use of
  student fees for nonpartisan political education activities.

° States should require student voting representation on state
  university boards of trustees.

° States should pass legislation ensuring the right of students
  to register and vote in their college communities.

Other

° States should establish programs to expand the university
  job retraining opportunities. Such programs can be especially
  valuable in communities hit by plant closings. New Jersey
  has established a program to expand job retraining through
  community colleges.

<u>FOR FURTHER INFORMATION</u>

<u>Publications</u>

Cognition, National Student Educational Fund, three times
a year, free. A newsletter examining policy issues affecting
students.

The College Student and Higher Education Policy: What
Stake and What Purpose, Carnegie Foundation for the Advancement of Teaching, 1975.

Policies for the Future: State Policies, Regulations and
Resources Related to the Achievement of Educational Equity for
Females and Males. Available from the Resource Center for Sex
Equity, Council of Chief State School Officers, 379 Hall of
the States, 400 N. Capitol St., N.W., Washington, D.C. 20001.

The Real Subminimum Wage, 1981. Includes material on
the student subminimum wage. Available for $2.50 from the
National Center for Jobs and Justice, 1638 R St., N.W.,
Washington, D.C. 20009.

<u>Organizations</u>

AMERICAN COUNCIL ON EDUCATION, 1 DuPont Circle, Washington,
D.C. 20036 (202) 833-4700. Comprises most the nation's colleges
and universities. A wealth of material on student financial
assistance and effects of the Reagan cutbacks. Publishes
Higher Education and National Affairs weekly ($30 per year).

AMERICANS FOR DEMOCRATIC ACTION YOUTH CAUCUS, 1411 K St.,
N.W., Washington, D.C. 20005 (202) 638-6447. Charlie King,
Director.

COALITION OF INDEPENDENT COLLEGE AND UNIVERSITY STUDENTS,
1730 Rhode Island Ave., N.W., Washington, D.C. 20036 (202)
659-1747.

NATIONAL COMMISSION ON STUDENT FINANCIAL ASSISTANCE, 412
First St., S.E., Washington, D.C. 20003. Will provide information on state student financial assistance programs.

NATIONAL STUDENT EDUCATIONAL FUND, 2000 P St., N.W., Room
300, Washington, D.C. 20036 (202) 785-1856. Kathy Downey,
President. Conducts research and organizing on student issues.
Has contacts for State Student Associations.

UNITED STATES STUDENT ASSOCIATION, 2000 P St., N.W., Room
305, Washington, D.C. 20036 (202) 775-8943. Janice Fine,
National Chair.

Prepared by David Jones.

The Governmental Process

Block Grants

BACKGROUND FACTS

One of the most important issues confronting state and local governments in the 1980s is the federal block grants.

The 1981 Omnibus Budget Reconciliation Act restructured many of the fiscal and programmatic relationships between the federal government and the states, consolidating 57 federal categorical aid programs into nine block grants.

Consolidation of categorical grants is only part of Reagan's plan to cut back federal assistance to states and cities. When Reagan handed the states the nine block grants, he also reduced funding for these programs by 25%. Colorado Governor Richard Lamm recently observed that block grants in their current form are actually "more authority to do less".

For example, although grants to state and local government account for only 10.7% of the total federal budget for FY 1983, they account for 26.3% of the proposed budget cuts. These FY 1983 cuts come on top of equally severe budget cuts in these same grants in FY 1982.

Needy citizens suffer most from Reagan's turn-back and cut-back approach to human service programs. Of the more than $35 billion cut, nearly $10 billion fell on families with incomes below $10,000 a year.

States have been put into a disastrous fiscal bind by the Reagan budgets. Most states must choose either to raise taxes to make up for federal cutbacks, or to cut services. An Associated Press survey of the fifty states found that:

° Eighteen have cut spending and/or raised taxes or settled for deficits exceeding $30 million or are facing such a choice;

° Twenty raised existing taxes or imposed new ones;

° Twenty states have laid off employees or stopped replacing those who leave. At least five also delayed or rejected raises for state workers.

<u>THE PROBLEM</u>

One of the major sources of funds for state and local governments in the 1980s will be the federal government. While President Reagan wants to dramatically cut the size of federal grants, federal money will continue to play a critical role in financing programs administered by the states.

Over the past two decades Congress has tried with some success to write into law important protections for the disadvantaged in federal grant programs to the states. Strong lobbying by liberal, civil rights, client groups, and others concerned about cost-effective, efficient programs built up strong protections to ensure that federal funds were used for the purposes that Congress had originally intended.

Protections written into many of the federal categorical grant programs included: 1) standards requiring public hearings and public participation in state decision making on federally-financed programs; 2) standard guidelines for regular evaluation of decision making; 3) regulations requiring state and local governmental compliance with civil rights law, accompanied by strong enforcement mechanisms; and 4) targeting of federally-financed programs to people most in need.

The Budget and Reconciliation Act of 1981 pushed through Congress by President Reagan and the Republican conservative Democrat coalition substantially weakened the protections added with such difficulty in the 1960s and 1970s. Federal guidelines covering the Block Grants are considerably weaker than the guidelines that had covered the previous 57 federal categorical grant programs. Regrettably, considerable Congressional pressure is growing that would further weaken or eliminate protections that survived the Budget and Reconciliation Act of 1981.

The pressure to weaken the Federal guidelines is heightened by the combined effects of the recession and the massive cutbacks in the amount of federal funds delivered to states and cities. States are increasingly tempted to view block grant funds as an extension of general revenue sharing funds, and thus use them for purposes that are only remotely related to the specific purposes of the block grant programs.

In the face of the continually-weakened federal guidelines for how federal funds should be spent, action by state governments is critical. New state legislation is needed which incorpoates progressive guidelines and standards similar to those that passed in the 1960s and 1970s. State action is critically needed at this point to insure that federal programs

are used in a manner consistent with the original congressional
purposes.

This action is needed in four interrelated areas involving
the nine federal Block Grant Programs. These four include:

Public Participation. Federal guideline in the budget
and Reconcilation Act of 1981 for public hearings and public
participation are extremely weak. Timely notice, wide publicity,
and regional meetings are important elements of public hearings.
Most states last complied with federal guidelines by holding
a single one-day hearing, covering all block grants. One-fourth
provided an opportunity for local governments, agencies, and
public interest groups to participate.

Evaluation and Accountability. New federal guidelines
do not require sufficient data collection and reporting to
permit effective evaluation either by the states or by the
federal government. State data collection has been poor in
the past. Because of the lack of acurate and sufficient
data, it will be impossible to trace the expenditure of
funds and to evaluate their impact.

Civil Rights Compliance. While each of the block grants
do contain "boilerplate" civil rights language, they do not
include any particular enforcement mechanism either for the
federal government or individual citizens in ensuring that
federal funds are spent in a non-discriminatory manner.
Requiring adherence to civil rights law is meaningless without
strong enforcement mechanisms built into the law.

Targeting Services to Needy Citizens. There is considerable danger that the once targeted federal grants programs
will disappear down the gullet of the state budget deficits.
The pressure on legislatures by politically powerful constituencies to use federal block grant funds for their own purposes
is already considerabble. Block grant funds may be shifted
away from specific program areas to more general ones, from
the poorest recipients and low-income communities to more
politically powerful ones, out of small-scale, community-
based, systems to larger, more established delivery systems.

<u>WHAT STATES CAN DO</u>

<u>Public Participation</u>

° States should create Block Grant Advisory Commissions to ensure public representation. They should include citizens directly affected by programs, nonprofit agencies serving principle beneficiaries, and state officials.

° States should be required to give adequate notice of public hearings on expenditure plans for block grants. The hearings should encourage active debate among citizens.

<u>Evaluation and Accountability</u>

° States should enact legislation providing for systematic data collection, accountability and evaluation of block grant expenditures.

° States should enact legislation ensuring that citizens will have access to the information needed to monitor and assess the state's plans and performances.

° States should enact legislation that provides for an evaluation of performance by local citizens. The evaluation should include a review of each project funded under the categorical programs and a determination as to whether they merit continued support.

<u>Civil Rights Compliance</u>

° States should enact, for each block grant, legislation prohibiting discrimination. This provision should assure that no person on the grounds of sex, religion, race, ethnic background, age or disability will be discriminated against under any program funded in whole or in part by federal block grant funds.

° States should enact legislation creating grievance procedures for the principal beneficiaries of block grant funds. Complaint hearings should be held before either an independent panel of citizens or a board of legislators.

<u>Targeting Services to Needy Citizens</u>

° States should enact legislation to ensure that the principal beneficiaries of these block grant programs are individuals in greatest need by reason of economic position, health, age, family circumstances and/or disabled condition.

° State shall enact legislation requiring that data be collected that will document the distribution of funds and program services to targeted populations.

Publications

Block Grants: A New Chance for State Legislatures to Oversee Federal Funds. Available from the National Conference of State Legislatures, Fiscal Affairs Program.

Briefing Book on Block Grants and the New Federalism. Coalition on Block Grants and Human Needs.

The Challenge of Block Grants: States Implement CSBG. Available from the Institute for Local Self-Government, Hotel Claremont Building, Berkeley, CA 94705.

A Children's Defense Budget: An Analysis of the President's Budget and Children, Children's Defense Fund, 1520 New Hampshire Ave., N.W., Washington, D.C. 20036.

Florida's Implementation of Federal Block Grants. Available from the Florida Advisory Council of Intergovernmental Relations, Lewis State Office Building, Suite 400, Tallahassee, FL 32304.

Preserving Community Development Block Grant Standards: A Model City Council Resolution from Albuquerque, NM, $2.50 from the Conference on Alternative State and Local Policies.

Testimony of Sandy Solomon before the Subcommittee on Intergovernmental Affairs, U.S. Senate, May 5, 1982. Available from the Coalition on Block Grants and Human Needs.

Organizations

CENTER ON BUDGET AND POLICY PRIORITIES, 236 Massachusetts Ave., N.E., Room 305, Washington, D.C. 20002.

COALITION OF BLOCK GRANTS AND HUMAN NEEDS, 1000 Wisconsin Ave., N.W., Washington, D.C. 20007 (202) 333-0822. Will provide information on state and federal block grant coalitions.

NATIONAL CONFERENCE OF STATE LEGISLATURES, FISCAL AFFAIRS PROGRAM, 1125 17th Street, 15th Floor, Denver, C.O. 80202 (303) 623-6600.

NATIONAL GOVERNOR'S ASSOCIATION, 444 N. Capitol St., Washington, D.C. 20001 (202) 624-5300.

Prepared by Barbara Pape.

Waste, Fraud and Abuse

Governmental accountability and competence was one of the biggest issues that concerned voters in the 1970s. This issue is also likely to rank high on the political agenda in the years ahead. Numerous polls indicate that the overwhelming majority of citizens are suspicious of government at all levels. They believe that corruption is widespread, that fraud and waste in government programs are common and that government programs and policies frequently do not achieve their intended result.

In 1978, for example, the Harris survey reported that 84% of all citizens believed that corruption and payoffs were common Moreover, that finding is consistent with previous polls.

Four years earlier the Harris survey determined that 60% of the respondents felt that local government corruption was a serious problem. In a Roper poll that same year, 58% of those surveyed said that most or many people in government took payoffs.

Other polls have found that citizens simply do not believe that government is competent -- that it can't solve the problems the nation faces. In 1976, for example, President Carter's pollster Patrick Caddell found that only 10% to 13% of all citizens believed that government "will actually be able to do" something about the nation's most pressing problems.

Unfortunately, the public's perceptions, while perhaps exaggerated, do have a strong basis in fact. Public corruption, while difficult to measure, appears to be widespread. A National Institute of Justice survey of the nation's newpapers has indicated that reports of official corruption can be found in all regions, though they are somewhat more common in the Northeast and North central regions than in the South and West. While most cases of reported corruptions came from cities (53%), suburbs and counties were not far behind (42%).

Federal prosecutions of public officials, another measure of the extent of public corruption, have increased substantially over the past ten years. The Justice Department's Public Integgrity Section reports that 211 local officials were convicted for federal crimes in 1981, up from 16 convictions in 1970. Last year 3,937 federal, state and local officials were convicted by federal prosecutors.

In dollar terms, the results of fraud and waste are staggering. In the late 1970s, Attorney General Benjamin Civiletti estimated that the government lost between $2.5 and $25 billion each year through fraud.

Throughout the past decade there has been a steady erosion of the public's confidence in its major institutions. Government officials face especially difficult problems in overcoming citizens' skepticism in the post-Watergate era. Public opinion polls repeatedly reflect the widespread perception that official corruption is pervasive. Furthermore, government programs to help the poor or assist in economic development are often viewed as being riddled with fraud.

Progressives have been outspoken advocates of more open government. They have led reform drives in many states to enact campaign election laws, provide for financial disclosure by public officials and pass open meetings legislation. These reforms are, in part, designed to deter official corruption which thrives on secrecy. Yet, generally, issues concerning fraud and waste in government programs have not been high on the list of progressive issues. Both official corruption and program abuse, especially abuse by service providers, are important problems that have contributed to the crisis of confidence that affects government. It is essential that those who design and support the goals of many government social programs take an active role in preserving the integrity of these programs.

Public corruption not only destroys citizens' faith in government, but also creates bitterness about their wasted tax dollars. Public corruption imposes a direct cost on taxpayers. Bid-rigging schemes raise the price of public contracts and can lead to an increase in taxes. A bribe to obtain a zoning variance -- from lower to higher population density, for example -- could mean that high-rise buildings are built where they do not belong. Schools become overcrowded, highways more congested and the general quality of life diminishes. And taxpayers pay the bill.

Corruption, of course, cannot be eliminated from public life. However, there are practical steps that government officials can take to deter public corruption and protect the integrity of government programs. One approach is designed to enhance government accountability by opening government decision-making to public scrutiny -- for example, campaign finance and financial disclosure laws. A second strategy involves implementing specific measures to reduce fraud, waste and abuse in goverment programs. This approach emphasizes the steps that can be taken to detect, investigate and prevent fraud and waste in goverment programs, such as by establishing Inspectors General (IGs) in agencies.

According to Common Cause, virtually all state courts
that have considered personal financial disclosure laws for
public officials have upheld their legality. Generally,
they have reasoned that the public's right to know outweighs
the need for privacy if the disclosure laws does not unduly
intrude into intimate personal matters.

There is little evidence that such laws deter many well-
qualified applicants from seeking office. Washington State,
for example, enacted a disclosure law in 1972 covering 272
elected state officials. Only one resignation has been attri-
buted to the laws.

Over the past few years many states have enacted legislation in the areas of campaign financing, conflict of interest
regulation and requiring open meetings.

Common Cause reports that there are now 47 states that
require candidates to file disclosure reports before elections. Individual contribution limits are in effect in 23
states. Seventeen states have enacted public financing for
state elections.

In the area of conflicts of interest, 44 states now require some form of financial disclosure by public officials.
Independent ethics commissions monitor and enforce those disclosure laws in 31 states.

All states now have open meetings laws and 45 states have
strengthened their laws over the past decade. Sanctions for
violating the open meetings laws are provided in 36 states.

Borrowing from the federal model, some states have created
Inspectors General (IGs) to coordinate efforts to prevent fraud
and waste. The use of "hotlines" provides a means by which
the public can report instances of program abuse. Vulnerability
Assessment has proven effective at the federal level. This
approach assesses a program's vulnerability to waste and fraud,
emphasizing prevention rather than investigation and detection.

Several arguments have been made against various open
government reforms. Campaign finance reforms that restrict
individual contributors, for example, have been attacked on
First Amendment grounds. Additionally, financial disclosure
has been challenged as an invasion of a public official's
privacy and on the basis that they would deter well-qualified
persons from seeking public office.

<u>WHAT STATES CAN DO</u>

<u>Open and Accountable Government</u>

° States should require quarterly reporting of all contributions to candidates seeking elected office. At a minimum,
reproting requirements should reflect guidelines used by the
Federal Election Commission.

° States should require the disclosure of personal and business
finances for all candidates for elected office and nominees
for major appointed office. Reports should reflect disclosure
of financial status for year prior to announcing for office
or being nominated.

° States should require public officials and major administrators to file financial disclosure reports reflecting the
above requirements at least once a year.

° States should review and, if necessary, amend existing legislation to ensure the public's right of access to government
records. The federal law provides a reasonably good model
for state legislation.

° States should enact legislation to protect public employee
whistle-blowers from reprisals. Michigan forbids employers
from discriminating against, threatening or firing employees
if the latter report or plan to report violations of federal,
state or local laws.

<u>Program Integrity</u>

° States should enact legislation to establish state Inspector
General offices based on the federal model. These officials
should be politically independent (for example, dismissed
only by the state's top executive) and have subpoena power.
Massachusetts and New York have established IG's through
legislation, although the IG's jurisdiction is limited.

° States should establish hotlines which allow citizens and
state employees to disclose instances of program abuse.
California, Washington and South Carolina use such hotlines,
and the California hotline is primarily designed to allow
state employees to disclose improper governmental activities.

° States should enact legislation allowing individual lawsuits
against fraud and waste. This would permit individual taxpayers to sue for the recovery of money for the government
when official enforcement is lax or inadequate.

<u>RESOURCES</u>

<u>Publications</u>

Fraud in Government Benefit Programs, J.A. Gardiner, et
al., National Institute of Justice, U.S. Department of Justice,
1982.

Anticorruption Strategy For Local Governments, T. Fletcher,
et al., Stanford Research Institute, Menlo Park, California,
1979.

Maintaining Municipal Integrity: Trainers Handbook, D.
Austern, et al., National Institute of Justice, U.S. Department
of Justice, 1980. Contains model legislation in the areas of
conflicts of interest, public contracting, open meetings and
the protection of public employees from retaliation.

<u>Organizations</u>

BETTER GOVERNMENT ASSOCIATION (BGA), 1901 Pennsylvania Ave.,
N.W., Washington, D.C., 20006, (202) 223-6164; and 230 N.
Michigan Ave., Chicago, IL, 60601, (312) 641-1181. The BGA
conducts investigations and publishes reports on governmental
performance.

COMMON CAUSE, 2030 M St., N.W., Washington, D.C., 20036, (202)
833-1200. State Common Cause offices are listed in the state
capital telephone directory.

PUBLIC CITIZEN LITIGATION GROUP, 2000 P St., N.W., Suite 700,
Washington, D.C., 20036. Has model state Freedom of Information legislation.

Prepared by Peter Manikas.

National Issues

Constitutional Amendments

<u>BACKGROUND FACTS</u>

The U.S. Constitution is an impressive document.

The Constitution has stood the test of time. It has served the nation well as the framework for a governmental system that has had to confront many varied situations and crises in our history.

Still, the framers of the Constitution understood that even the best-crafted document in the world would need to be modified occasionally to meet changing societal needs. They therefore included amending procedures that offer two routes for proposing amendments and two routes for ratifying them.

Since it was written in 1787, the U.S. Constitution has been amended 26 times. Many of these expanded the rights and obligations for American citizens. The Fourteenth Amendment, for example, gave freed slaves the right to vote, and the Nineteenth, passed in 1920, extended suffrage to all American women. In some instances, Constitutional amendments were adopted to bring about greater efficiency and democracy in government (such as those dealing with the succession of office and the direct election of federal legislators).

The Constitution (Article V) provides two routes for proposing amendments and two routes for ratifying them. Amendments can be proposed by a two-thirds affirmative vote of Congress; or, by a constitutional convention, called by Congress, at the request of two-thirds (34) of the state legislatures. Amendments initiated by either process can then be ratified either by the state legislatures or state conventions in three-fourths (38) of the states in order to achieve final adoption. Of the 26 constitutional amendments adopted so far, all have been approved first by Congress and then by the states.

A constitutional convention has not been called since the nation's founders met in Philadelphia in the late 18th century to initially amend the Articles of Confederation and ended up drafting an entirely new Constitution. While several attempts since then have been made to call a convention, all have failed.

<u>THE PROBLEM</u>

In all likelihood, one of the biggest set of issues that
America's state legislatures will face in the next two years
will be constitutional amendments. State legislators will
face politically controversial and even explosive votes
regarding if and how the United States Constitution should
be amended.

On the one hand, the New Right is proposing Constitutional
amendments in three key areas: requiring a balanced budget,
permitting prayer in the public schools, and prohibiting
abortion. These issues may reach the state legislatures in
1983 if Congress approves them. In addition, the New Right
is also trying to pass the balanced budget amendment by
calling a Constitutional Convention.

On the other hand, women's, civil rights, labor and
other organizations have reintroduced the Equal Rights Amendment into Congress. If Congress passes it again, the state
legislatures could receive that in 1983 as well.

The New Right inspired amendments represent an attempt
to make constitutional issues out of partisan social or
political policy issues. This is the case with proposed
amendments calling for prayer in the schools, an end to
school busing, and the outlawing of abortions. In addition,
the amendment calling for a balanced federal budget represents
an attempt to alter the Constitution to provide a temporary
political solution to questions of federal fiscal policy.

<u>"Balanced" Budget</u>. Congress is now considering such a
constitutional amendment for submission to the state legislatures. Such an amendment might reach the state legislatures
in January 1983 at the beginning of the session.

Conservative supporters of a constitutional amendment
requiring a balanced budget are also trying another strategy
to get their amendment approved. They have gone to the states
directly, asking them to call on Congress to call a Constitutional Convention to approve the amendment. Thirty-four
states are needed; they now have 31.

Apart from the merits of the issues, the Constitutional
Convention raises many legal and constitutional questions.
Critics of the Constitutional Convention charge that without
established guidelines on how many amendments can be raised,
proponents of specific political views could turn the convention
into a free-for-all that could leave the entire Constitution
up for grabs. In addition, many feel that issues which have
heretofore been dealt with in the legislative realm, such as
school prayer and busing, will be arbitrarily included in the
Constitution.

National Issues

    <u>School Prayer</u>. President Reagan submitted a proposed
constitutional amendment on prayer the public schools in May
1982. The Senate will hold hearings in the summer of 1982,
and it could reach the floor of the Senate by the end of the
year. If supporters could get it out of Committee, the
amendment could pass the House of Representatives and reach
the state legislatures in 1983.

    The campaign behind this amendment has been described by
some as an attempt to launch a "crusade to recover the Holy
Grail from the un-Christian Supreme Court". This highly
charged, political measure has been attacked by conservatives
and liberals alike.

    The amendment clearly is an attempt by right wing, and
in many cases, fundamentalist Christian, groups to sponsor
group prayer in the schools, prayer that by many opinions
would impose one religious standard over another. This was
often the case in the pre-Supreme Court decision days, when
Jewish children, among other religious minorities, were
often subjected to recitation of the Lord's Prayer in a
majority Christian classroom.

    <u>Prohibition on Abortion</u>. In every session of Congress
since the U.S. Supreme Court decision of 1973 legalizing
abortion, legislation or proposed constitutional amendments
have been introduced to effectively overturn that decision.
On the legislative side, Senators Jesse Helms (R-NC) and
Mark Hatfield (R-OR) have introduced separate pieces of
legislation that would effectively outlaw abortion by legislat-
ing that life begins at conception. Thus, abortion would
be homicide under prevailing criminal law.

    The proposed constitutional amendment was drafted and
submitted by Senator Orrin Hatch (R-UT). He would amend the
Constitution by affirming that both Congress and the states
have the power to regulate and/or prohibit abortion. The
Hatch amendment will reach the floor of the Senate in the
summer of 1982. On the House side, it remains bottled up in
committee.

    <u>Equal Rights Amendment</u>. The ERA was first introduced
in Congress in 1973, and was defeated June 30, 1982, lacking
three states for ratification. The ERA was reintroduced in
Congress in July 1982 and Congress will probably consider it
again in 1983. It could reach the state legislatures in
1983 or 1984.

    The main text of the proposed Equal Rights Amendment is
as follows: "Equality of rights under the law shall not be
denied or abridged by the United States or by any State on
account of sex."

<u>WHAT STATES CAN DO</u>

<u>Balanced Budget</u>

° State legislatures should reject the proposed constitutional
  amendments requiring a "balanced budget" if Congress
  passes one and submits it to the states.

° State legislatures which have passed resolutions calling
  for a constitutional convention for a balanced budget should
  rescind their resolution.

<u>School Prayer</u>

° State legislatures should reject any proposed amendment on
  legalizing organized school prayer if Congress passes
  such an amendment and submits it to the states.

<u>Abortion</u>

° State legislatures should reject any proposed constitutional
  amendment which would allow the Congress or the states to
  prohibit or limit a woman's right to choose if Congress
  passes such an amendment and submits it to the states.

<u>Equal Rights Amendment</u>

° State legislatures should ratify the Equal Rights Amendment
  if Congress passes the amendment and submits it to the
  states.

<u>FOR FURTHER INFORMATION</u>

<u>Balanced Budget</u>

AFL-CIO, 815 16th Street, N.W., Washington, D.C. 20006
(202) 637-5289.

LEAGUE OF WOMEN VOTERS, 1730 M Street., N.W., Washington,
D.C. 20036 (202) 296-1770.

NATIONAL EDUCATION ASSOCIATION, 1201 16th Street, N.W.,
Washington, D.C. 20036 (202) 83-4000.

<u>Constitutional Convention</u>

THE COMMITTEE TO PRESERVE THE CONSTITUTION, 225 West 34th
St., Suite 1500, New York, NY 10001.

<u>Abortion</u>

PLANNED PARENTHOOD FEDERATION OF AMERICA, 1220 19th Street.,
N.W., #303, Washington, D.C. 20036 (202) 347-8500.

NATIONAL ABORTION RIGHTS ACTION LEAGUE, 1424 K Street., N.W.,
Washington, D.C. 20005 (202) 347-7774.

RELIGIOUS COALITION FOR ABORTION RIGHTS, 100 Maryland Ave.,
N.E., Washington, D.C. 20002 (202) 543-7032.

<u>School Prayer</u>

NATIONAL EDUCATION ASSOCIATION, 1201 16th Street., N.W.,
Washington, D.C. 20036 (202) 833-4000.

AMERICANS UNITED FOR SEPARATION OF CHURCH AND STATE, 8120
Fenton Street, Silver Spring, MD 20910 (301) 589-3707

AMERICAN CIVIL LIBERTIES UNION, 132 West 43rd Street, New
York, NY 10036 (212) 944-9800.

<u>Equal Rights Amendment</u>

NATIONAL ORGANIZATION FOR WOMEN, 425 13th Street, N.W.,
Washington, D.C. 20004 (202) 347-2279.

NATIONAL WOMEN'S POLITICAL CAUCUS, 1411 K Street., N.W.,
Washington, D.C. 20005 (202) 347-3078.

LEAGUE OF WOMEN VOTERS, 1730 M Street., N.W., Washington,
D.C. 20036 (202) 785-2616.

Prepared by Linda Tarr-Whelan.

Nuclear Weapons Freeze

BACKGROUND FACTS

In just half an hour, every city in the Northern Hemisphere could be destroyed by the arsenal of 50,000 nuclear weapons possessed by the United States and the Soviet Union.

Yet, over the next decade, both countries plan to build at least 20,000 more nuclear warheads, missiles, and aircraft.

These rapidly escalating numbers have alarmed hundreds of thousands of Americans. Growing concern about the threat of a nuclear holocaust has led to a groundswell of support for a "freeze" of existing U.S.-Soviet nuclear weapons. this proposal has aroused more American support than any arms control issue since the end of World War II.

Areas of "high risk" -- likely targets in the event of a Soviet nuclear attack -- are located in every state in the nation. Industrialized urban centers are primary targets; however, less populous states may also be targeted if they contain major military installations.

The freeze movement began to gather momentum in November 1980. Efforts have been directed on a state-by-state basis with activity occuring at various levels of government.

Legislatures in Oregon, Connectitut, Maine, Vermont, Minnesota, Delaware, Iowa, and New York have passed resolutions calling for an immediate halt to the nuclear arms race. In addition, the Maryland, Alaska and Illinois State Senates and the Kansas and Pennsylvania Houses of Representatives have expressed support for a freeze. This fall citizens in California, Michigan, Rhode Island, New Jersey, and Wisconsin, will vote on freeze resolutions. Citizens in Arizona, Michigan, and Washington D.C. have collected the necessary signatures, but freeze resolutions await final ballot approval.

At the local level, freeze resolutions have been introduced and passed in over 200 city councils and fourty-three county commissions. Both the U.S. Conference of Mayors and the National Conference of State Legislatures have passed endorsement resolutions.

On March 10, 1982, Senators Edward Kennedy (D-MA) and Mark O. Hatfield (R-OR), introduced a joint resolution calling for a "mutual and verifiable freeze" on testing, deployment, and production of warheads and their delivery systems with "major, mutual reductions" to follow.

Arms control and nuclear war are two of the most critical issue facing our nation. Public officials at all levels of government are becoming active around the freeze.

Although public support for a freeze resolution is now substantial and growing, the idea of a weapons freeze is not new. Both the Johnson and Nixon Administratons considered freeze proposals, and the idea resurfaced in 1979 during the Carter Administration, when the President proposed a freeze on production and deployment of nuclear weapons to Leonid Brezhnev.

The freeze movement has been growing rapidly, and popular support continues to expand. Generally, the freeze's critics have been unsuccessful in stopping or preventing the movement from expanding.

However, critics continue to argue against a freeze. They make two major arguments that they believe proves that the freeze is a bad idea.

The first argument that the critics make is that the United States trails the Soviet Union in nuclear weapons strength and a freeze at existing levels would leave the U.S. at a disadvantage.

Supporters of the freeze agree that the Soviet Union does have an advantage in the total number of launchers (ICBM's) with very heavy throw-weights (total size of payload); but argue that that advantage is not important. The United States' strength is still superior because of other "nuclear weapons delivery systems."

Proponents of the freeze claim that any "vulnerability" of the US ICBM force is more than offset by a U.S. advantage in the other two legs of the strategic triad -- Submarine-Launched Ballistic Missiles, which are less vulnerable to attack than land-based missiles, and heavy bombers now being equipped with extremely effective cruise missiles.

Supporters of the freeze would also agree that the Soviet Union has more intermediate range nuclear forces in Europe than NATO forces, if one only counts ground-based missles. NATO is at least equal to, if not superior, to the Soviet Union if one counts all intermediate range nuclear weapons deployed in and around Europe. The critics fail to consider the U.S. and British sea-launched weapons assigned to NATO and the French _force de frappe_.

The second major argument of the critics is that the Soviet Union cannot be trusted to comply with the freeze and the
U.S. does not have adequate means to verify whether they do
comply or not. Freeze supporters say that this argument is
false. They point out first of all that their proposal calls
for an agreement based on mutual verification in all stages
of testing, deployment, and production and presumes that
adequate technology exists to assure such a verification.

Verification technology does exist and it can definitely
work. Freeze advocates point out that because of the reli-
ability of verification tests of delivery systems and warheads,
any Soviet violation of a freeze almost certainly would be
discovered before the less verifiable production stage occurs.
Thus, they contend, the whole system can be monitored effectively.

A freeze on testing of delivery systems and warheads
can be monitored with elaborate satellite detection systems
for missiles and seismographic instruments for warhead tests.
In the case of small cruise missiles, designed to fly close
to the ground (which only the U.S. has developed), verification
of testing would be more difficult, though still possible,
given the highly sensitive overhead surveillance capabilities
of our satellites and air reconnaissance systems.

A freeze on deployment of new weapons is the easiest
thing of the three to monitor. Large delivery systems are
difficult to conceal from overhead surveillance. Bombers,
land-based missiles, and submarine-launched missiles are
readily visible to satellites. Cruise missile deployment
can be checked through controls on the number and loading
capacity of air, naval and ground platforms and launching
systems. This procedure was successfully incorporated into
the SALT II agreement.

A freeze on production is perhaps the hardest aspect of
arms control to verify, though its is still possible. Freeze
advocates believe that the U.S. has sufficient knowledge of
Soviet production plant locations to enable it to monitor
activity by infra-red sensors on satellites (which detect
the heat emitted in an active plant). On-site inspection is
necessary only once -- to certify a plant's deactivation.
Thereafter, ordinary satellite observation can detect efforts
to re-establish production at the deactivated facility.
Attempts to build new plants can also be discovered through
such means.

<u>WHAT STATES CAN DO</u>

° States should pass resolutions calling for an immediate
  freeze and mutually verifiable reductions in the testing,
  production, and further deployment of nuclear weapons,
  missiles, and other delivery systems in the U.S. and Soviet
  Union.

° States should pass legislation that would refuse to allocate
  state funds, staff time, or facilities to civil defense
  planning. Such state resources should only be earmarked
  for other types of emergency disaster situations.

° States should pass resolutions calling upon Congress to
  divert tax dollars spent on nuclear weapons and other unnecessary military spending to jobs and other human services.

° States should modify their economic development plans
  towards diversifying economies that significantly depend on
  military contracts. States should consider matching funds
  with state military contractors to finance feasibility
  studies for such diversification.

FOR FURTHER INFORMATION

Publications

A "Jobs with Peace" Budget: A Model Resolution for States
and Cities, Legislative Brief, $2.50 from the Conference on
Alternative State and Local Policies.

Freeze! How Can You Prevent Nuclear War? Senator Edward
Kennedy and Senator Mark Hatfield, 1982. Bantam Publishing
Co. $3.50.

Civilian Defense form Nuclear War Information Packet,
1982, Civil Defense Awareness, 22 Lowell Street, Cambridge,
MA 02133. Packet contains articles on various civil defense
rejection activities around the country.

Questions and Answers on the Soviet Threat and National
Security. $ .75. American Friends Service Committee, 1501
Cherry St., Philadelphia, PA 19102. Answers questions about
the Soviet "military buildup." A useful guide for people
gathering signatures or addressing the public on the nuclear
freeze.

Rejecting Crisis Relocation Plans: The Cambridge, Massachusetts Ordinance, $2.50 from the Conference on Alternative
State and Local Policies.

Organizations

CENTER FOR DEFENSE INFORMATION, 122 Marlyand Ave. N.E.,
Washington, D.C., 20002 (202) 484-9490.

COMMITTEE FOR NATIONAL SECURITY, 2000 P St., N.W., Washington,
D.C., 20036 (202) 833-3140. A non-profit, non-partisan
leadership group which promotes debate on the nature of
national security and how best to achieve it.

PHYSICIANS FOR SOCIAL RESPONSIBILITY, P.O.Box 144, 23 Main
St., Watertown, MA, 02172 (617) 491-2754. An organization
of health professionals and concerned citizens dedicated to
professional and public education on the medical consequences
of nuclear weapons and war.

NUCLEAR WEAPONS FREEZE CAMPAIGN NATIONAL CLEARINGHOUSE,
4144 Lindell Blvd., Suite 404, St. Louis, MO, 63108
(314) 533-1169. Updated state and local activity around the
nation. Also includes contact names and addresses of freeze
organizers in every state.

Prepared by Victoria Baldwin and Ann Cahn.

List of Contributors

<u>Victoria Baldewin</u> (NUCLEAR WEAPONS FREEZE) is a research
 assistant at the Joint Economic Committee of the U.S.
 Congress.

<u>Joseph Belden</u> (AGRICULTURE) is a staff member of the
 Center for Study of Social Policy.

<u>Barbara Bode</u> (CHILD CARE) is president of the Children's
 Foundation.

<u>Fred Branfman</u> (INDUSTRIAL INNOVATION) is Director of Research
 for the Governor's Office of the state of California.

<u>Jeff Brummer</u> (UTILITIES) is Utilities Clearinghouse
 Coordinator with the Electric Utilities Project of the
 Environmental Action Foundation.

<u>Ann Cahn</u> (NUCLEAR WEAPONS FREEZE) is executive director of
 the Committee for National Security.

<u>Joanna Chusid</u> (THE ELDERLY) is senior legislative assistant
 at the National Council of Senior Citizens.

<u>Elliot Currie</u> (CRIMINAL JUSTICE) is a sociologist who has
 taught criminology at Yale and the University of California.
 He is currently working with the California Governor's
 Task Force on Civil Rights.

<u>Ann Evans</u> (COOPERATIVES) directs the Cooperative Development
 Program of the California Department of Consumer Affairs.

<u>Donald Fraher</u> (HANDGUN CONTROL) is legislative director for
 Handgun Control, Inc.

<u>John Froines</u> (WORKPLACE SAFETY AND HEALTH) is former director
 of occupational health for the state of Vermont and former
 deputy director of the National Institute for Occupational
 Safety and Health. He is currently a faculty member of
 the School of Public Health at the University of California
 at Los Angeles.

<u>Lennie Goldberg</u> (HOUSING) is a legislative staff specialist for
 California Assemblyman Tom Bates.

<u>Derek Hansen</u> (SMALL BUSINESS) is president of Derek Hansen
 and Associates, Inc.

Marilee Hanson (HOUSING) is a housing consultant in Oakland,
California.

Edward Hopkins (WATER AND SEWERS) is research director of the
Clean Water Action Project.

Robert Hunter (INSURANCE) is executive director of the National
Insurance Consumers Organization.

David Jones (PLANT CLOSINGS, STUDENTS) is the editor of Ways
and Means at the Conference on Alternative State and Local
Policies.

William Jordan (NUCLEAR POWER) is a partner with the law firm
of Harmon & Weiss.

Debbie Kaplan (CITIZENS WITH DISABILITIES) is a staff attorney
at the Disability Rights Education and Defense Fund.

Peter Lafen (ENVIRONMENTAL PROTECTION) is transportation counsel
at the Friends of the Earth.

Linda Lampkin (PUBLIC EMPLOYEES) is director of research at
the American Federation of State, County and Municipal
Employees.

James Lewis (TOXICS) is editor of Exposure, the publication of
the Waste and Toxic Substances Project at the Environmental
Action Foundation.

Peter Manikas (WASTE, FRAUD AND ABUSE) is legislative counsel
and chief of the Washington, D.C. office of the Better
Government Association.

Richard Munson (SOLAR AND ENERGY CONSERVATION) is executive
director of the Solar Lobby.

David Olsen (PENSION FUND INVESTMENT) is former executive
director of the New School for Democratic Management.
He is currently treasurer of the San Francisco Public
Pension Investment Project.

Barbara Pape (BLOCK GRANTS) is a research associate at the
Conference on Alternative State and Local Policies.

Anthony Robbins (HEALTH CARE) is former director of the National
Institute for Occupational Safety and Health, and is currently
president-elect of the American Public Health Association.

Michael Samuels (CIVIL RIGHTS) is executive director of the Ohio
   Civil Rights Commission.

William Schweke (LABOR LEGISLATION, PLANT CLOSINGS) is managing
   editor of The Entrepreneurial Economy at the Corporation
   for Enterprise Development.

Richard Spohn (CONSUMER PROTECTION) is director of the
   California Department of Consumer Affairs.

Larry Swift (BANKING) is president of the Woodstock Institute.

Linda Tarr-Whelan (CONSTITUTIONAL AMENDMENTS, PUBLIC EDUCATION,
   WOMEN) is director of government relations at the National
   Education Association.

David Wilhelm (TAX REFORM) is a research specialist with the
   Public Employee Department of the AFL-CIO.

Bob Zdenek (COMMUNITY ECONOMIC DEVELOPMENT) is president of
   the National Congress for Community Economic Development.

David Zwick (WATER AND SEWERS) is executive director of the
   Clean Water Action Project.